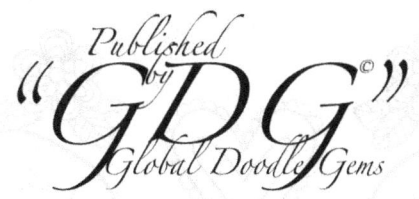 

Colors of Whimsy II

Again, I could not have done this without
the love and patience of my husband, Frank, and family
Many thanks to Maria, my publisher and friend.
Also, many thanks and much appreciation goes
also to Debbie Lai for putting me in touch with her
neice Jennifer Rainbow and the Taiwan Team and the
beautiful job they did of coloring my drawings.

Please check out these other books:
Colors of Whimsy
Global Doodle Gems Series

You can find me on Facebook at
http://www.facebook.com/bevchoyart

or by email
bevchoy70@gmail.com

Copyright 2015 Colors of Whimsy II
All rights are reserved by Bev Choy. Duplication of pages for personal use are allowed.
You are invited to color the pages then scan/post your colored versions to social networks,
mentioning the book title and author/artist (Colors of Whimsy II).
All artwork and images are protected by copyright laws. This book or any portion therof
may not, otherwise, be reproduced and/or distributed or transmitted without the express written
permission of the artist/publisher of Colors of Whimsy II.

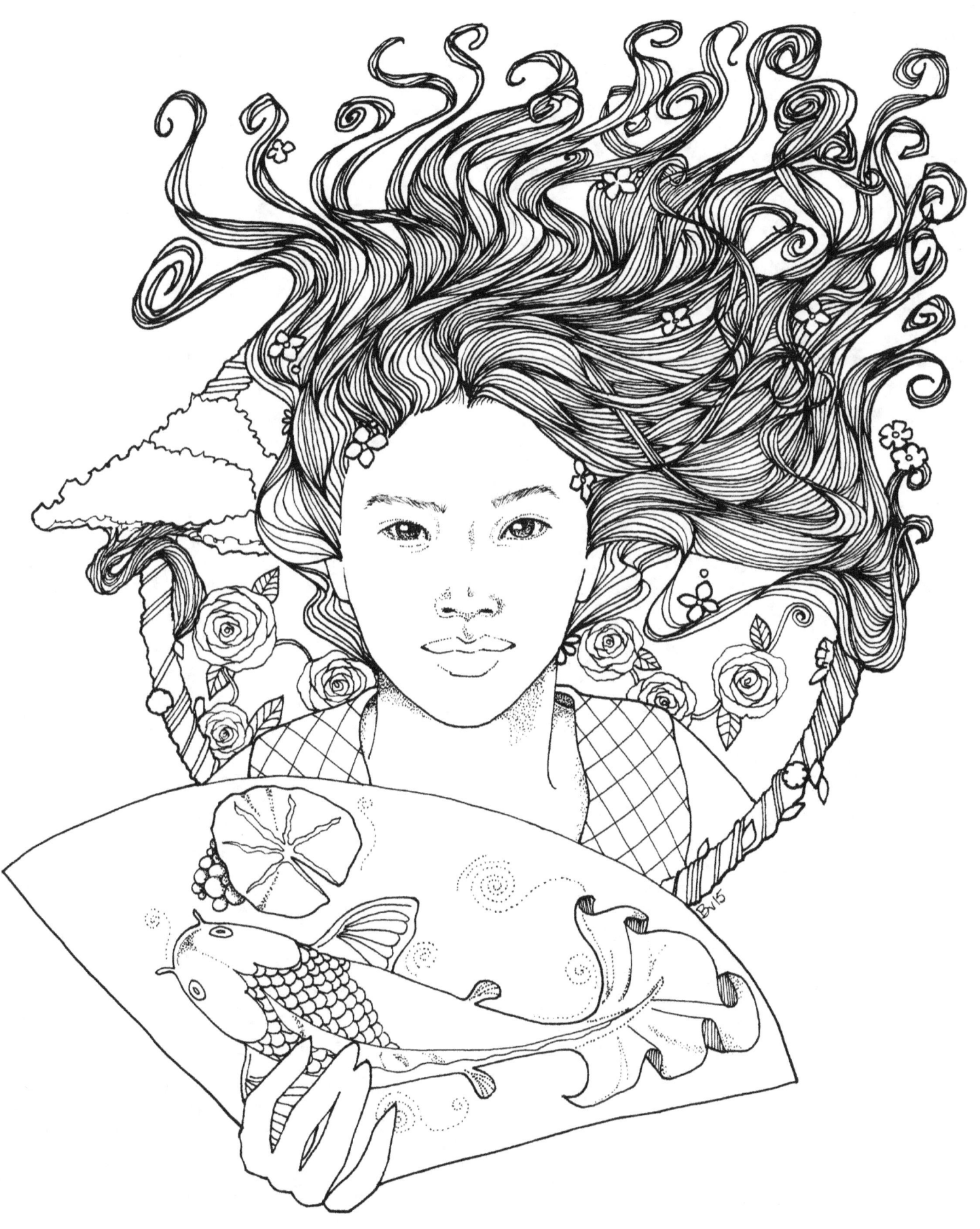

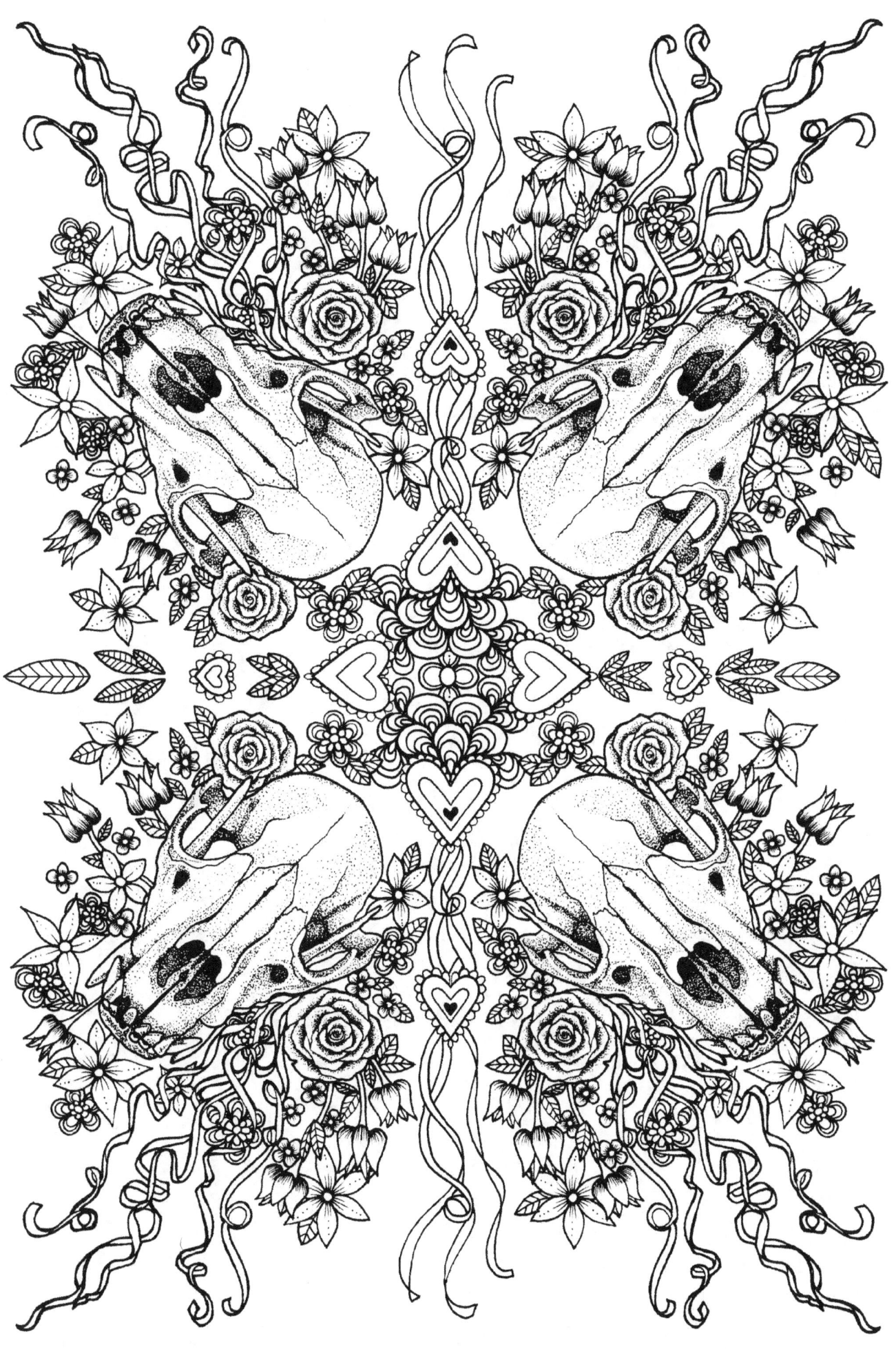

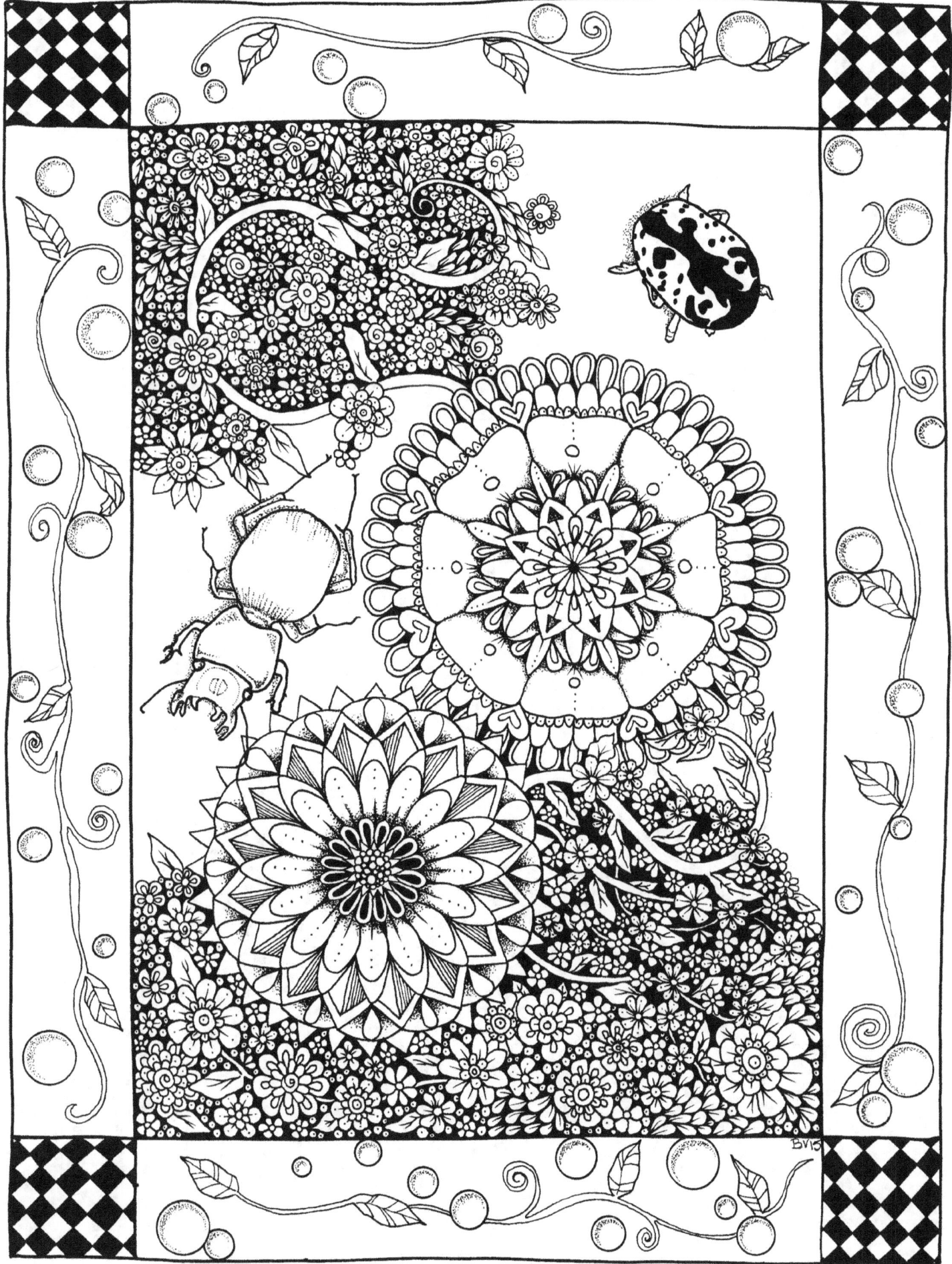

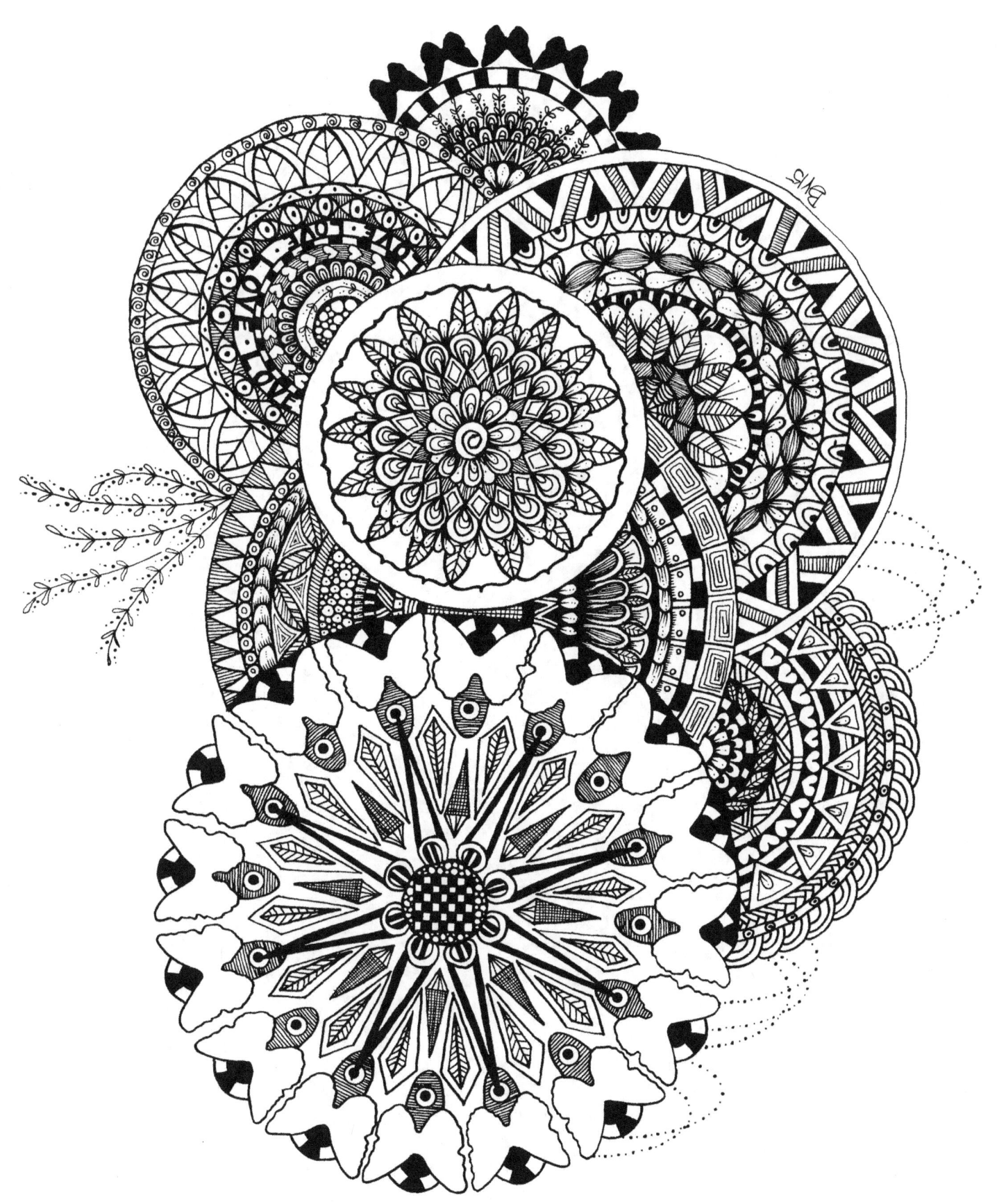

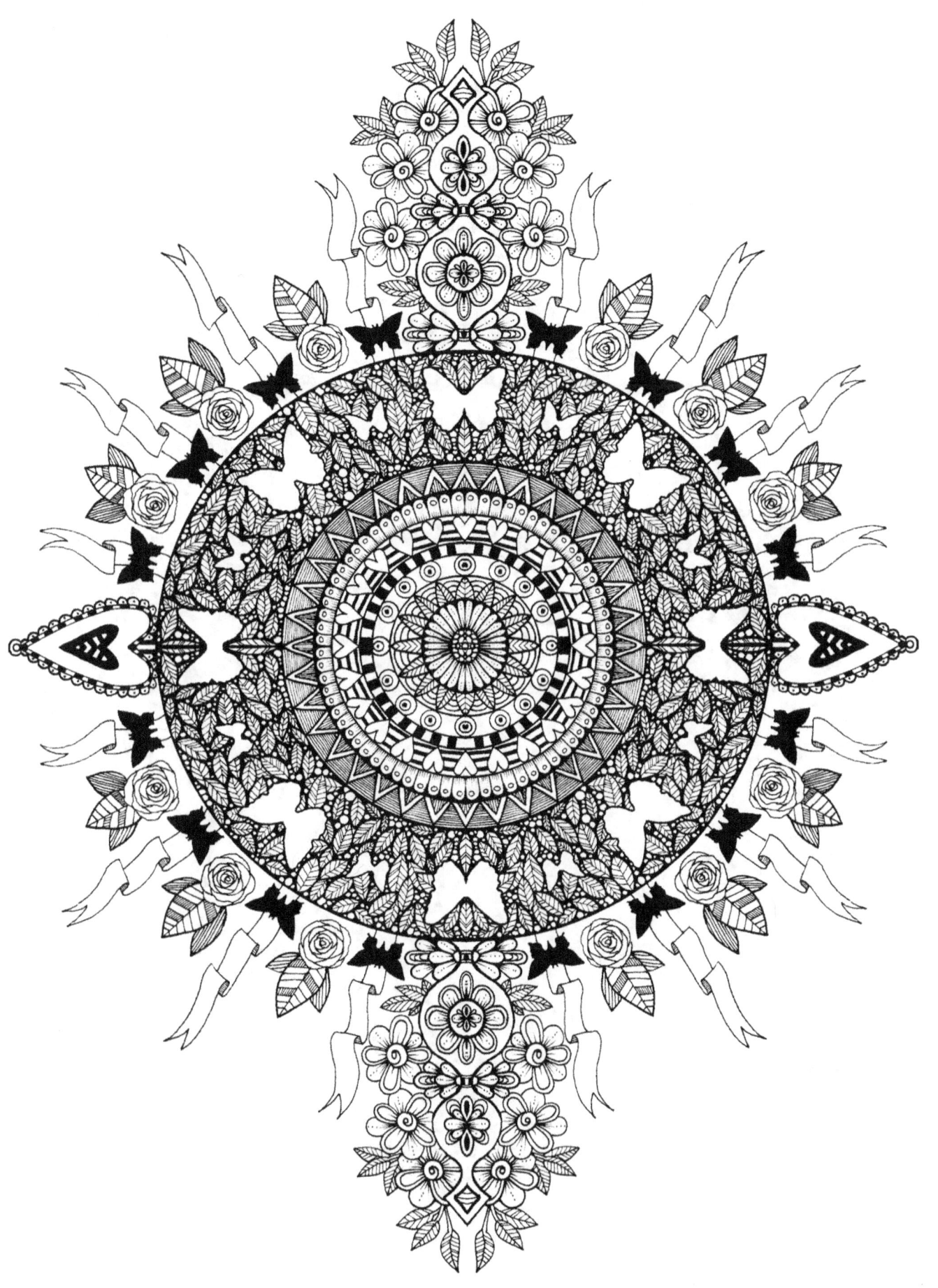

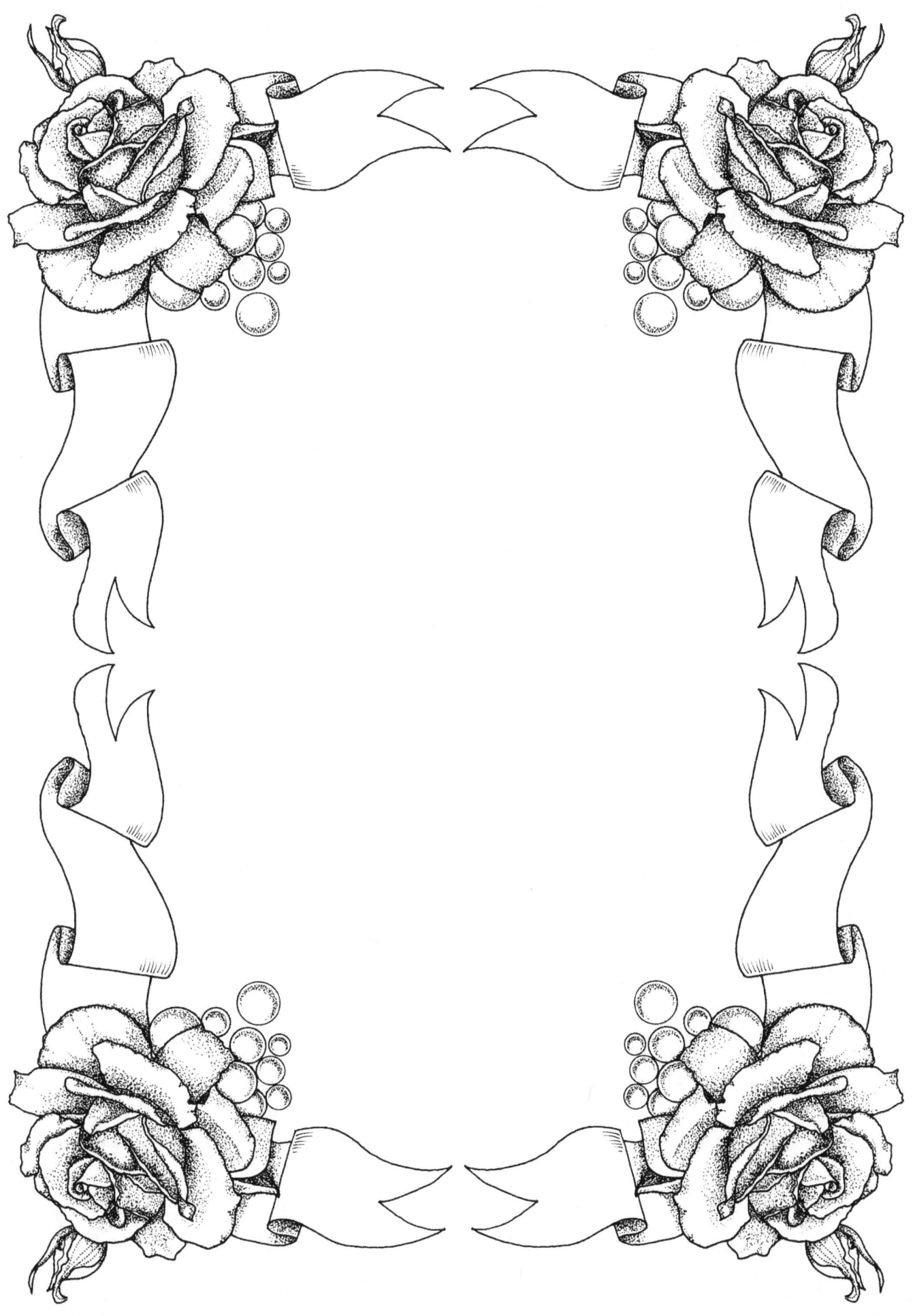

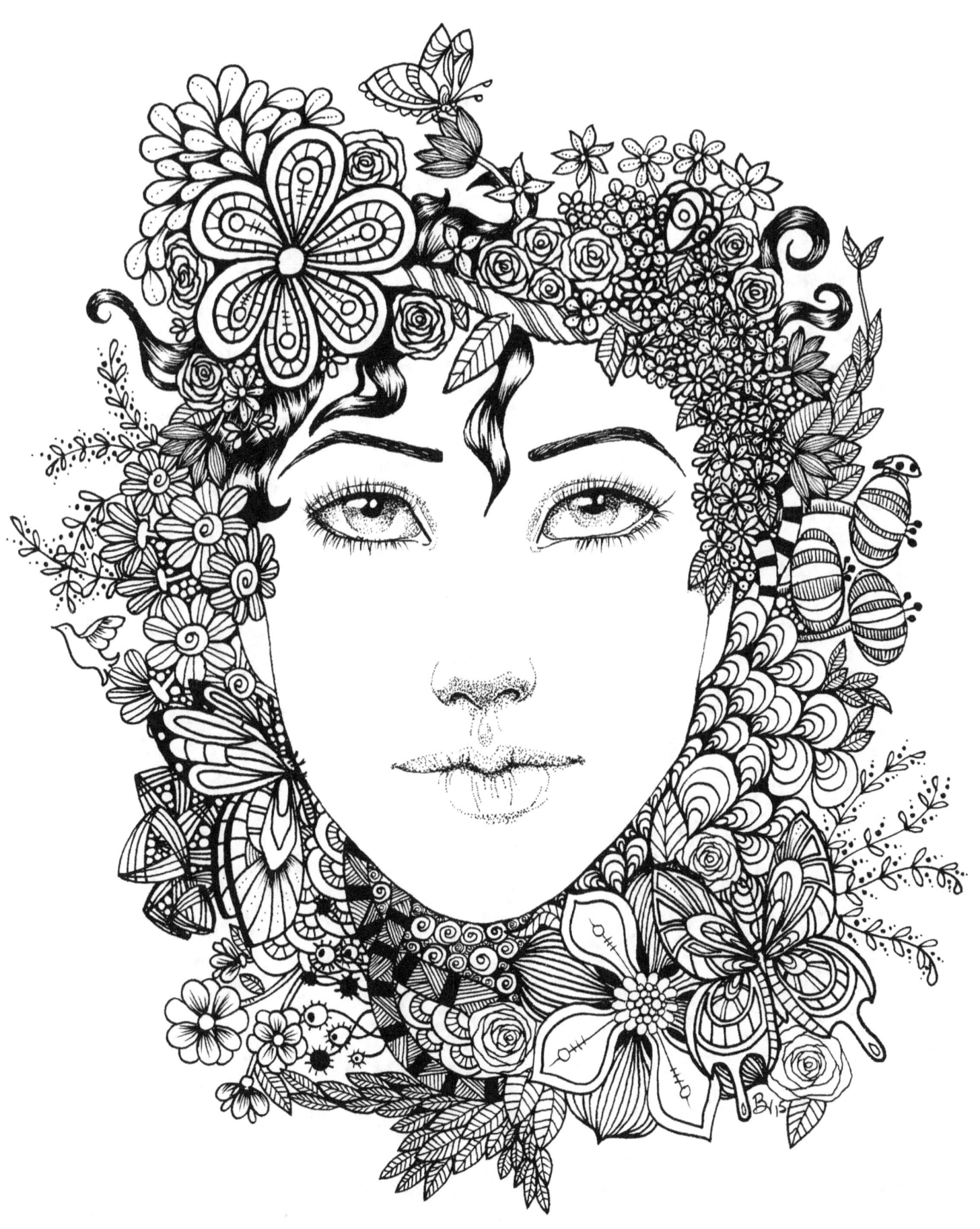

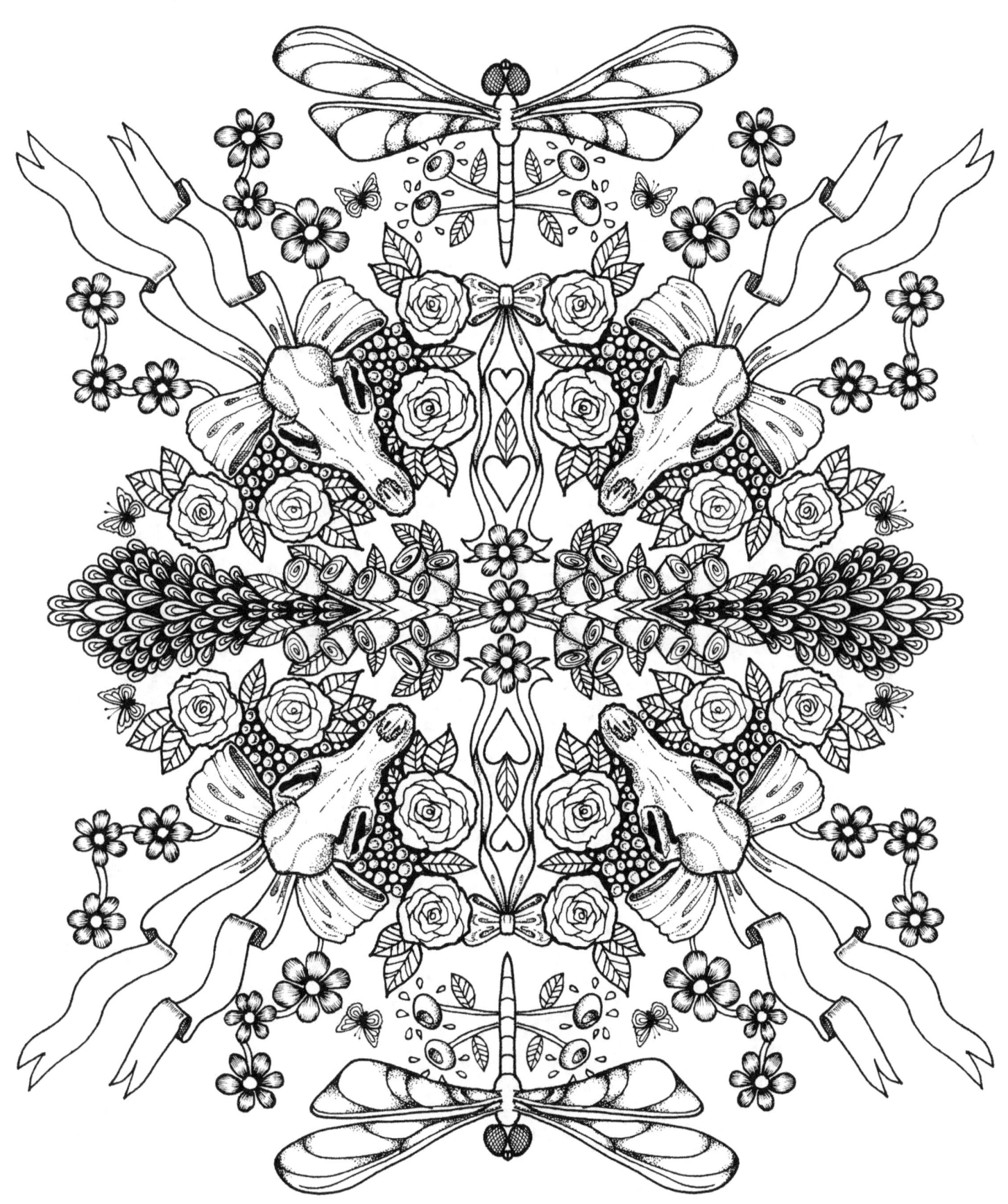

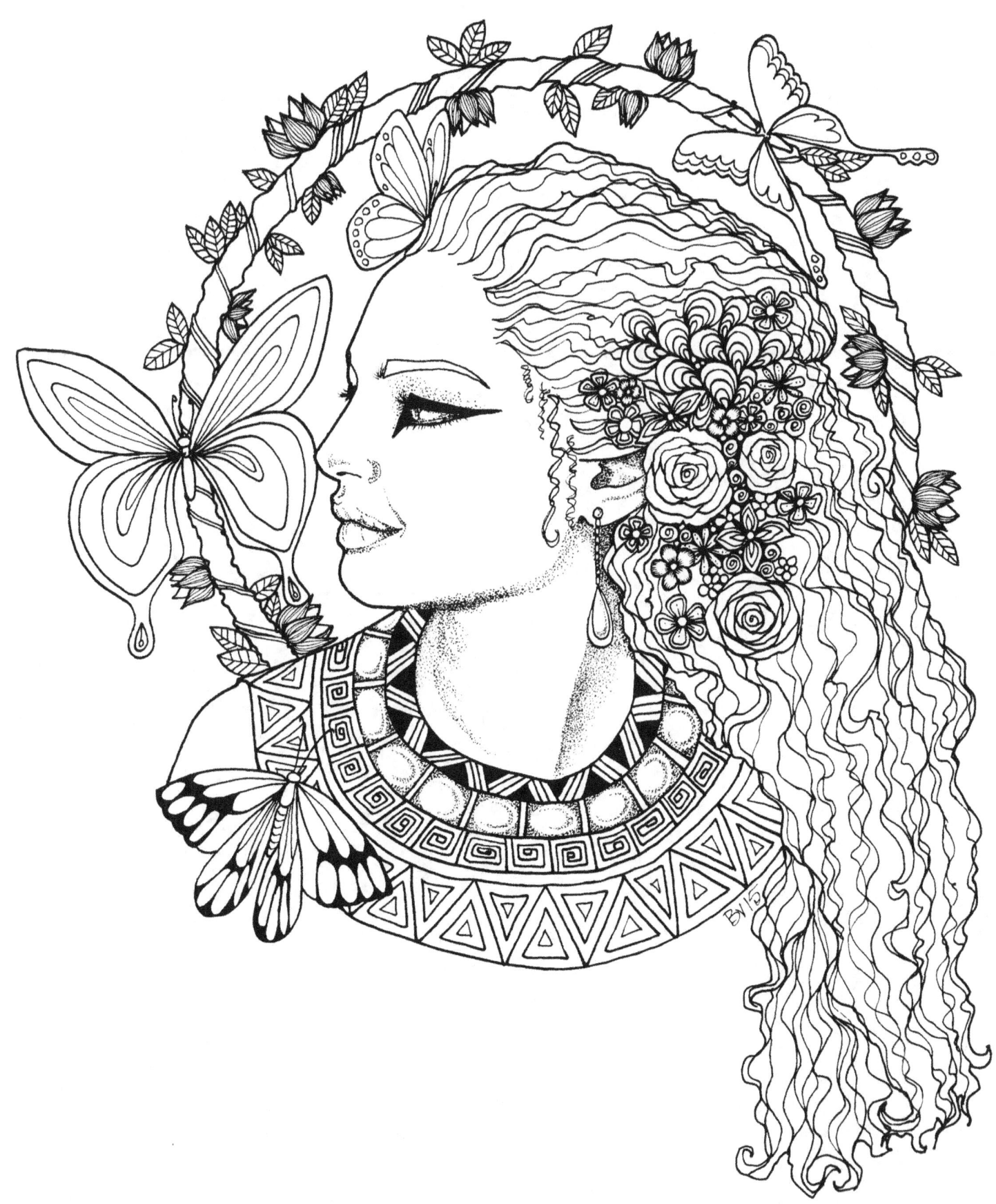

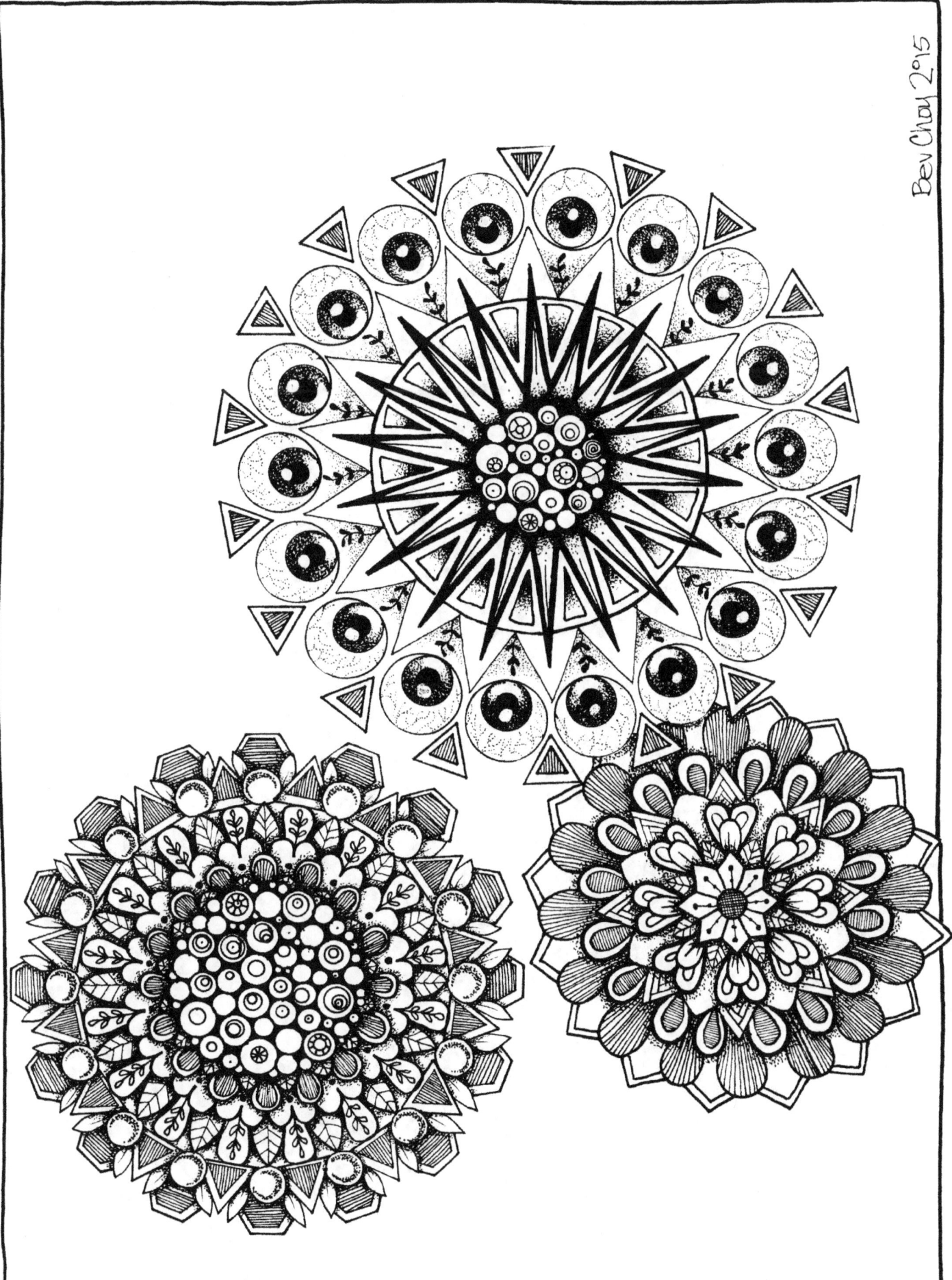

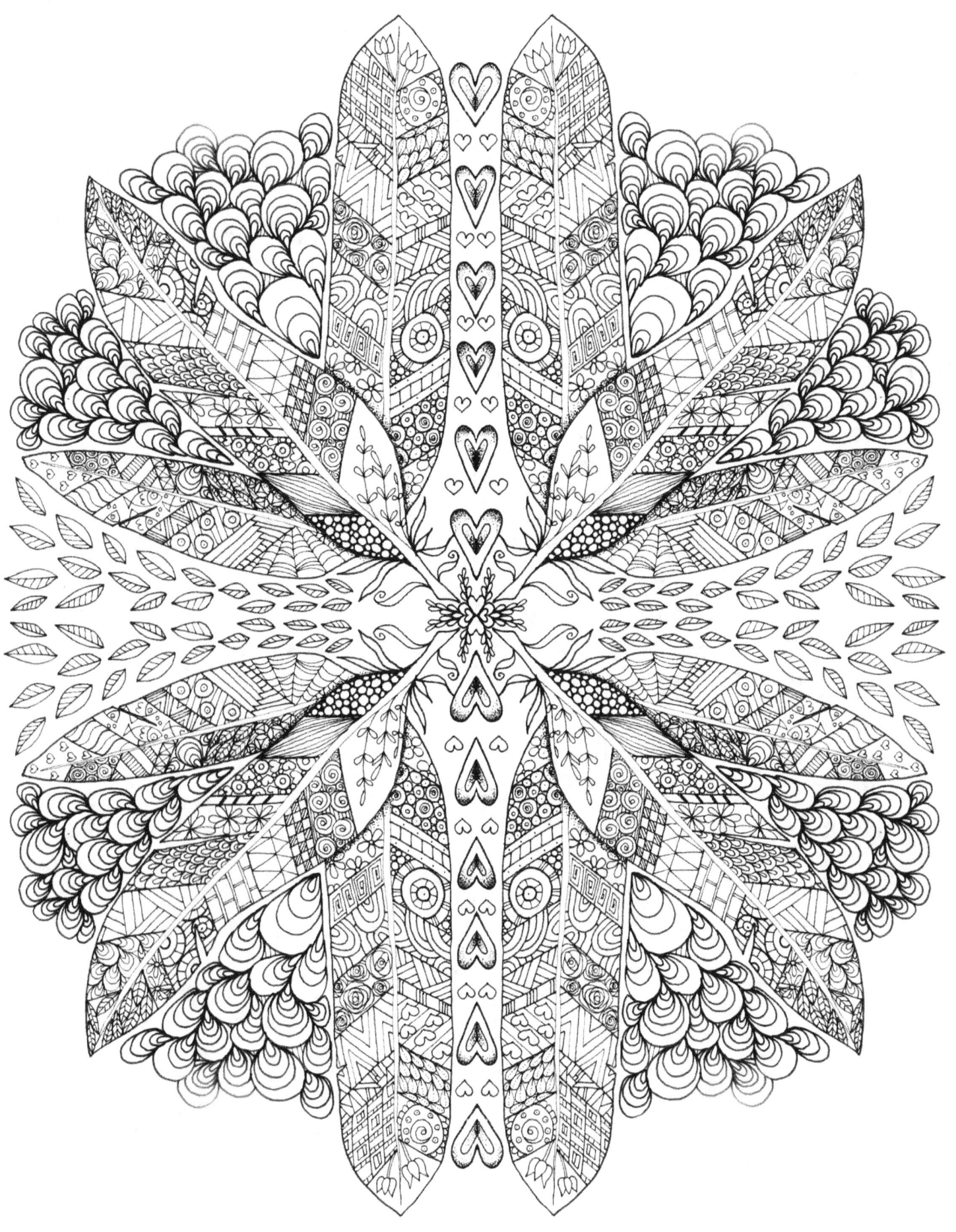

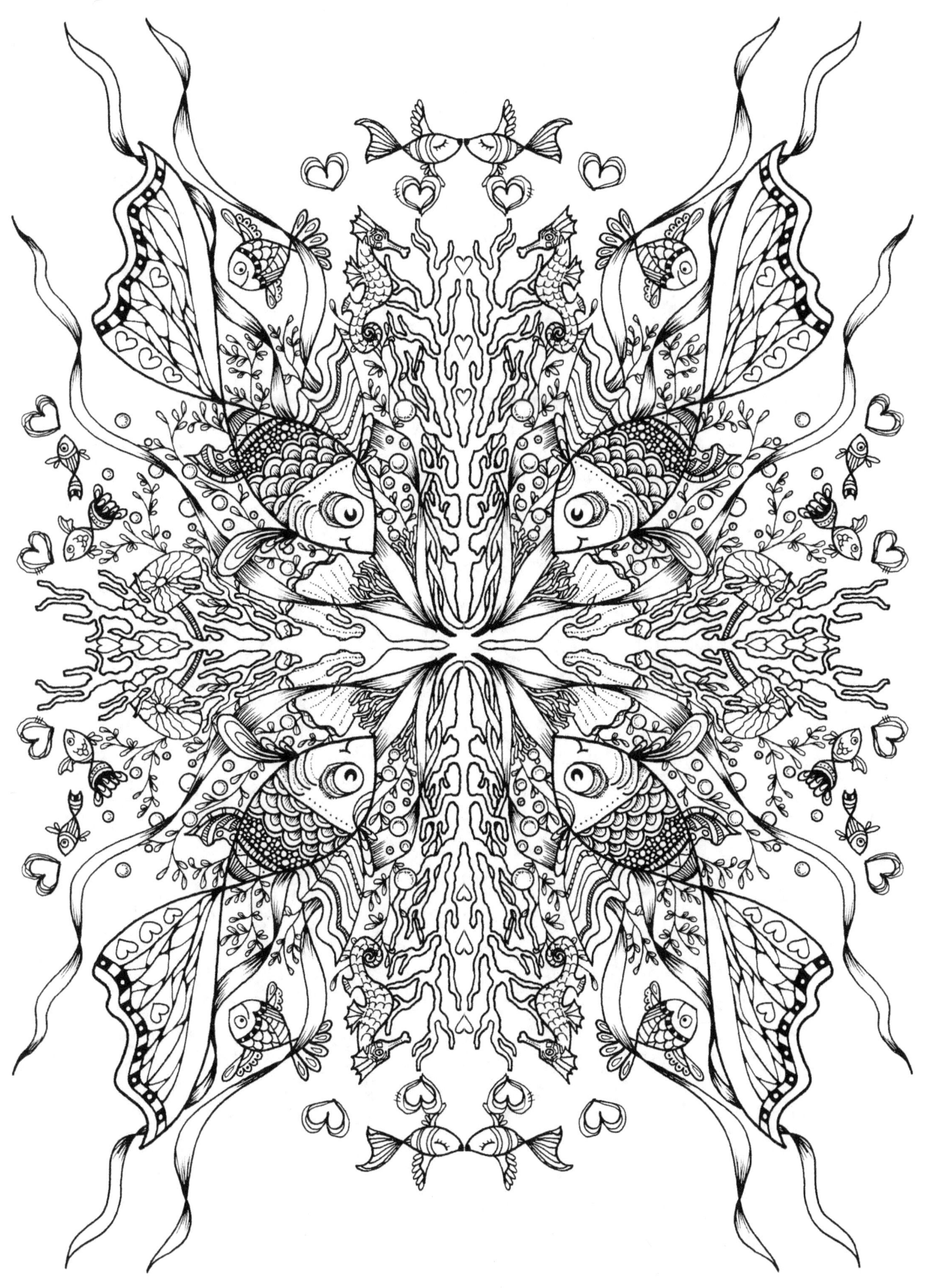

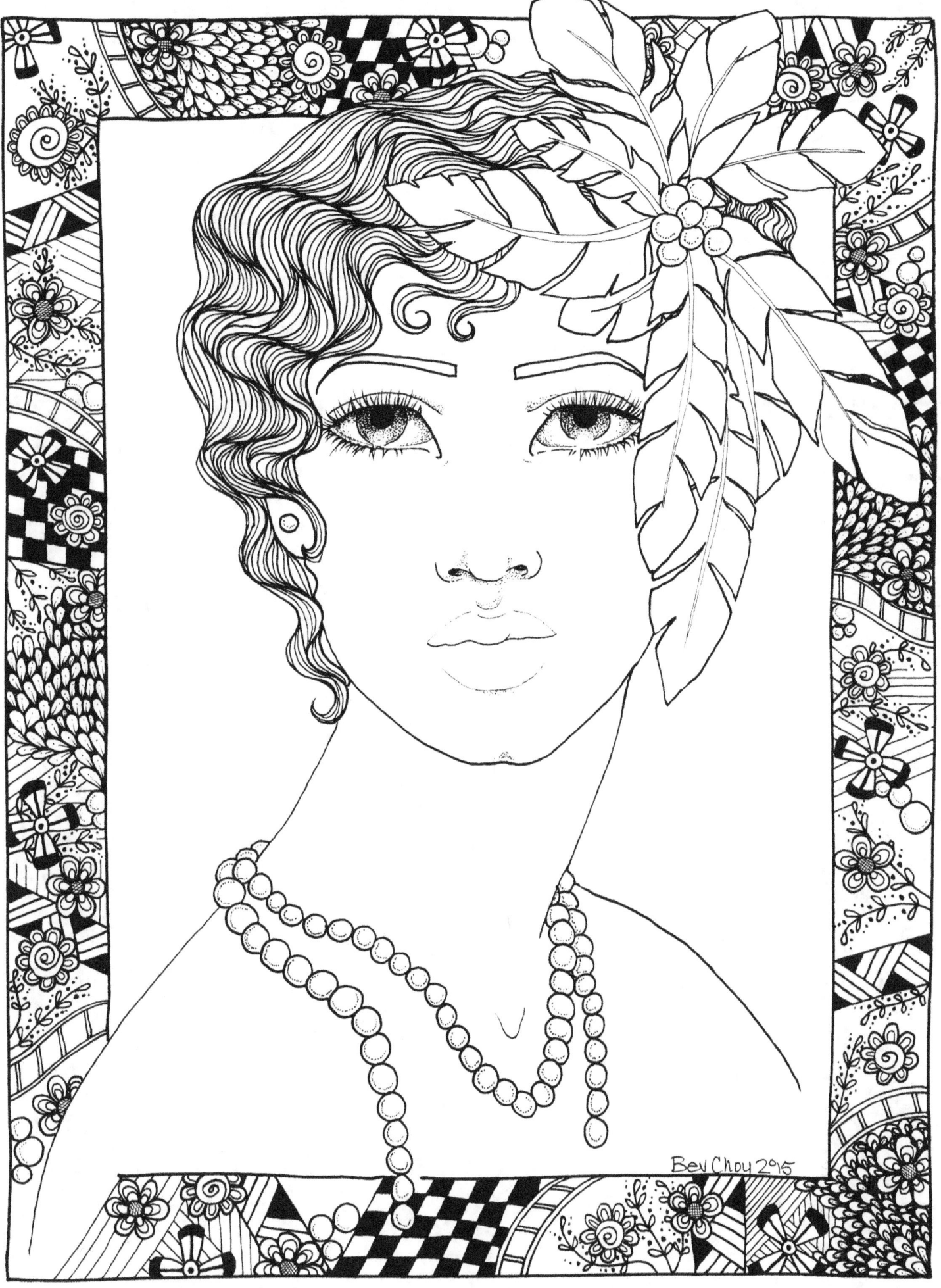

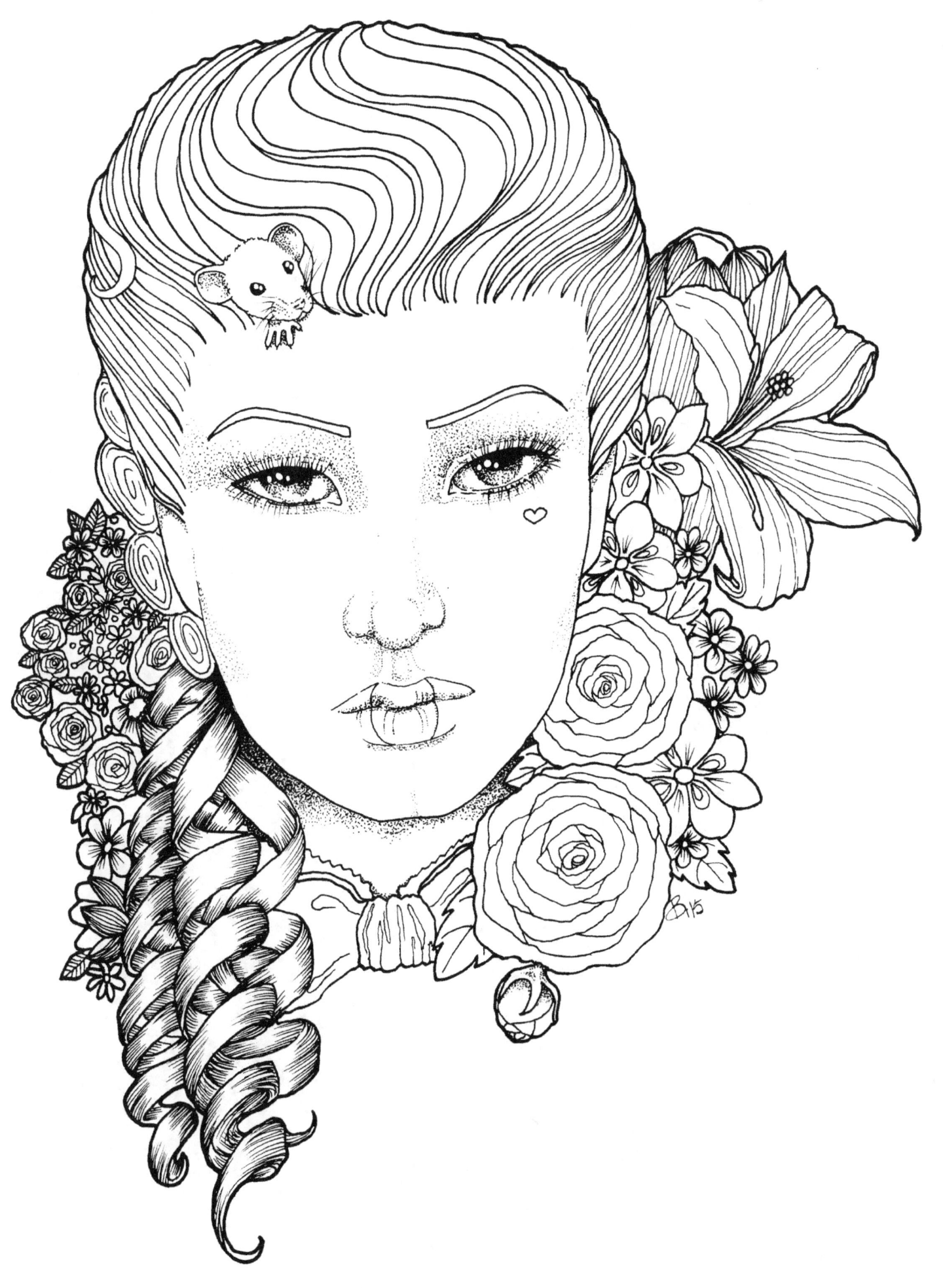

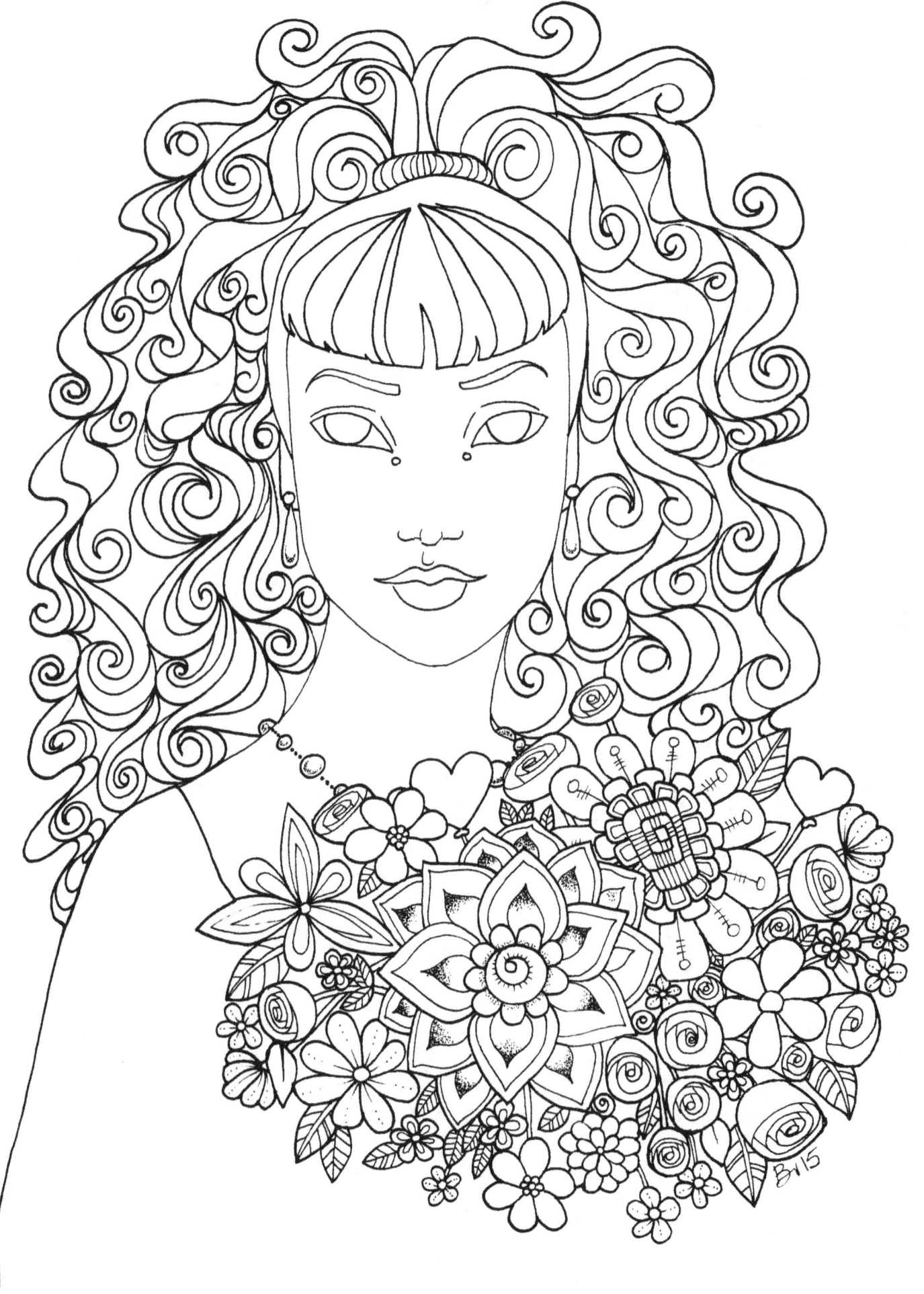

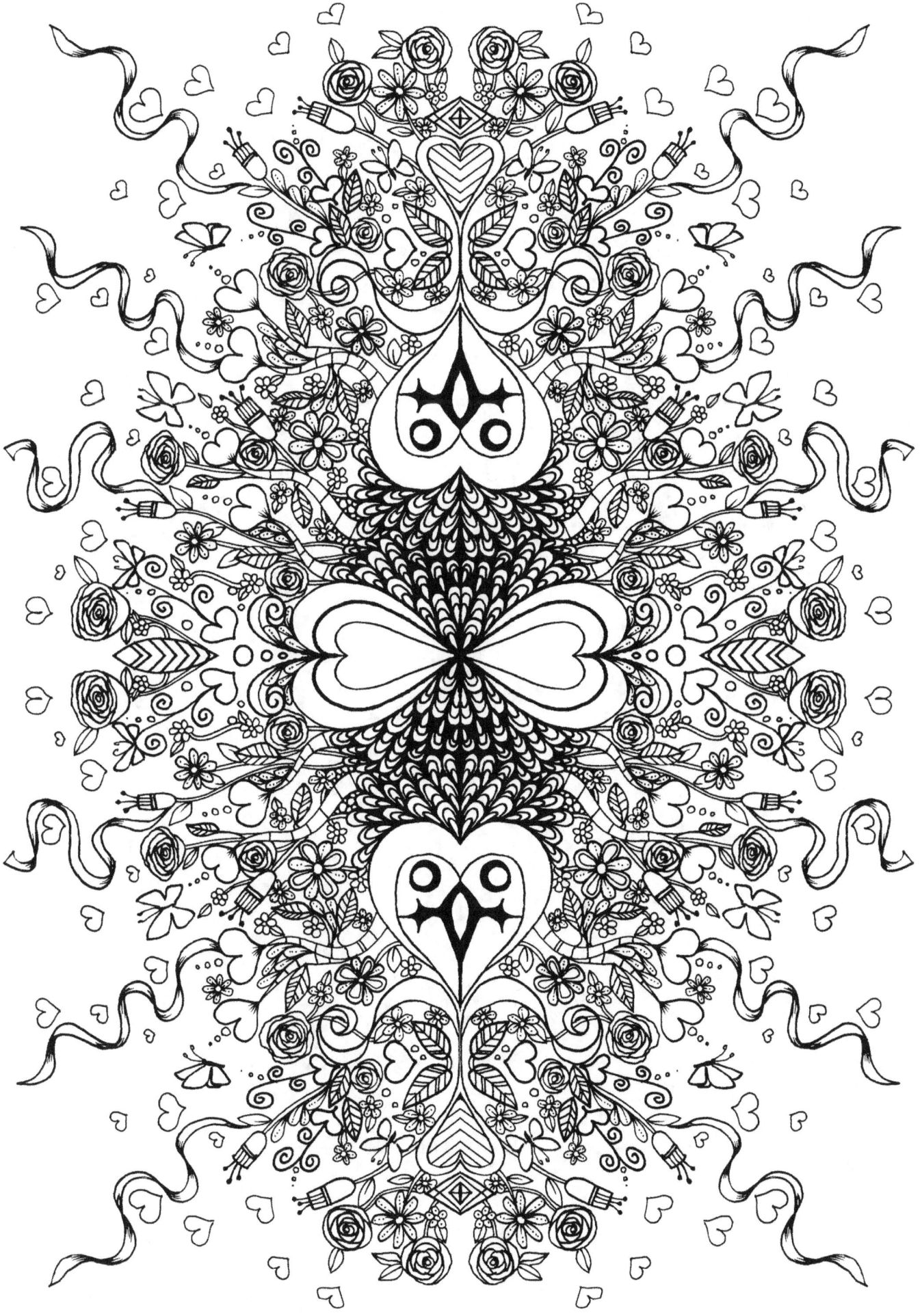

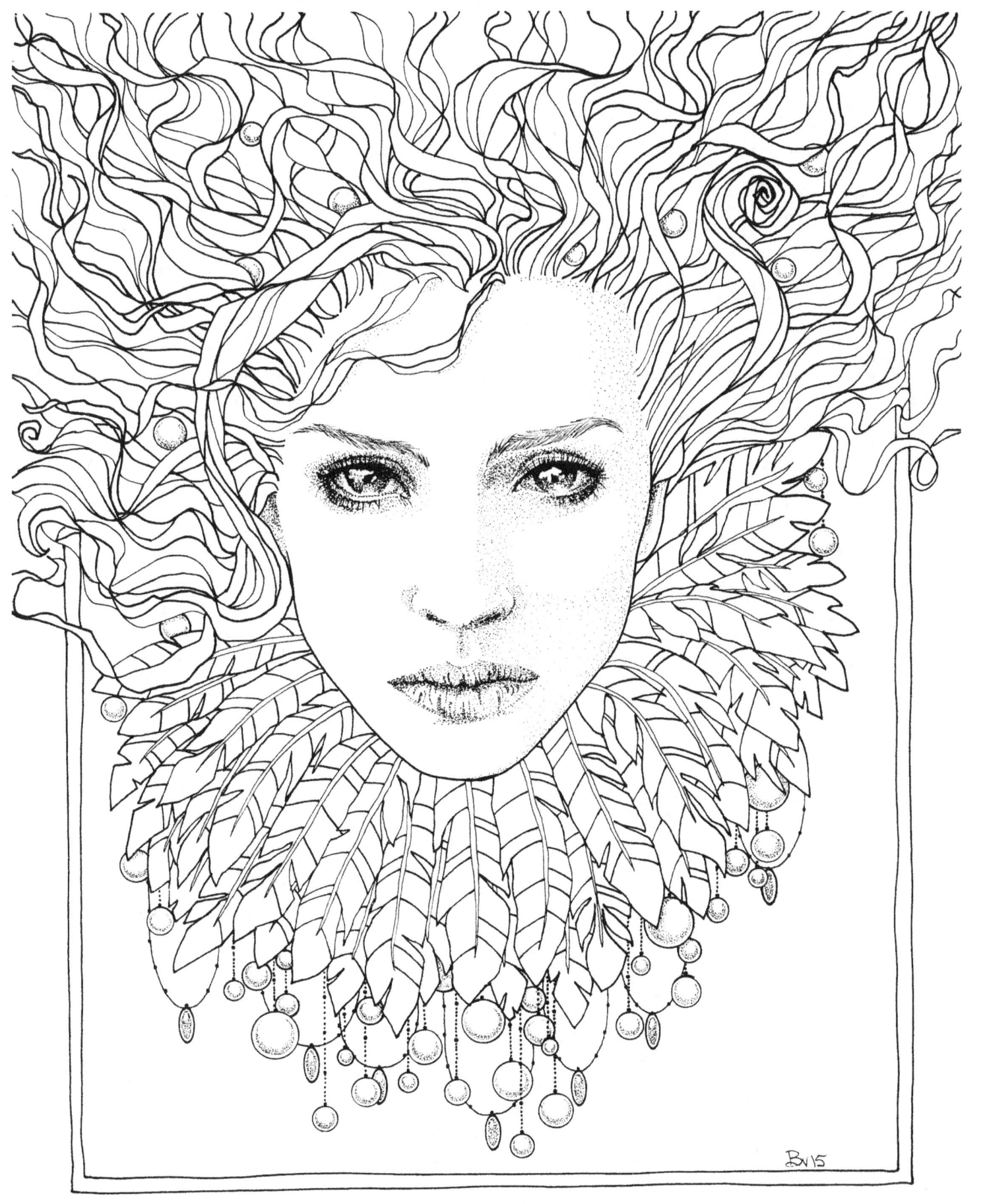

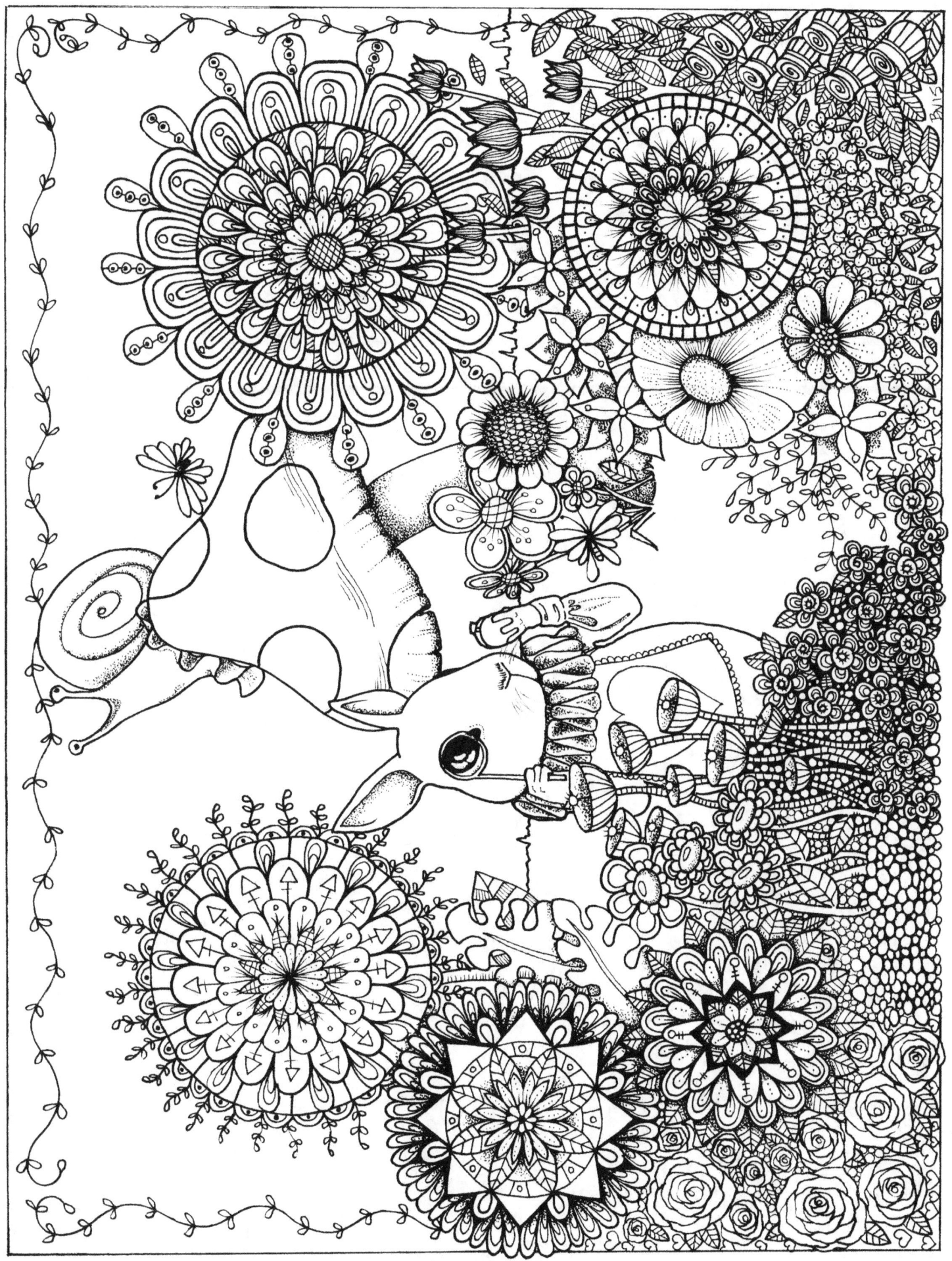

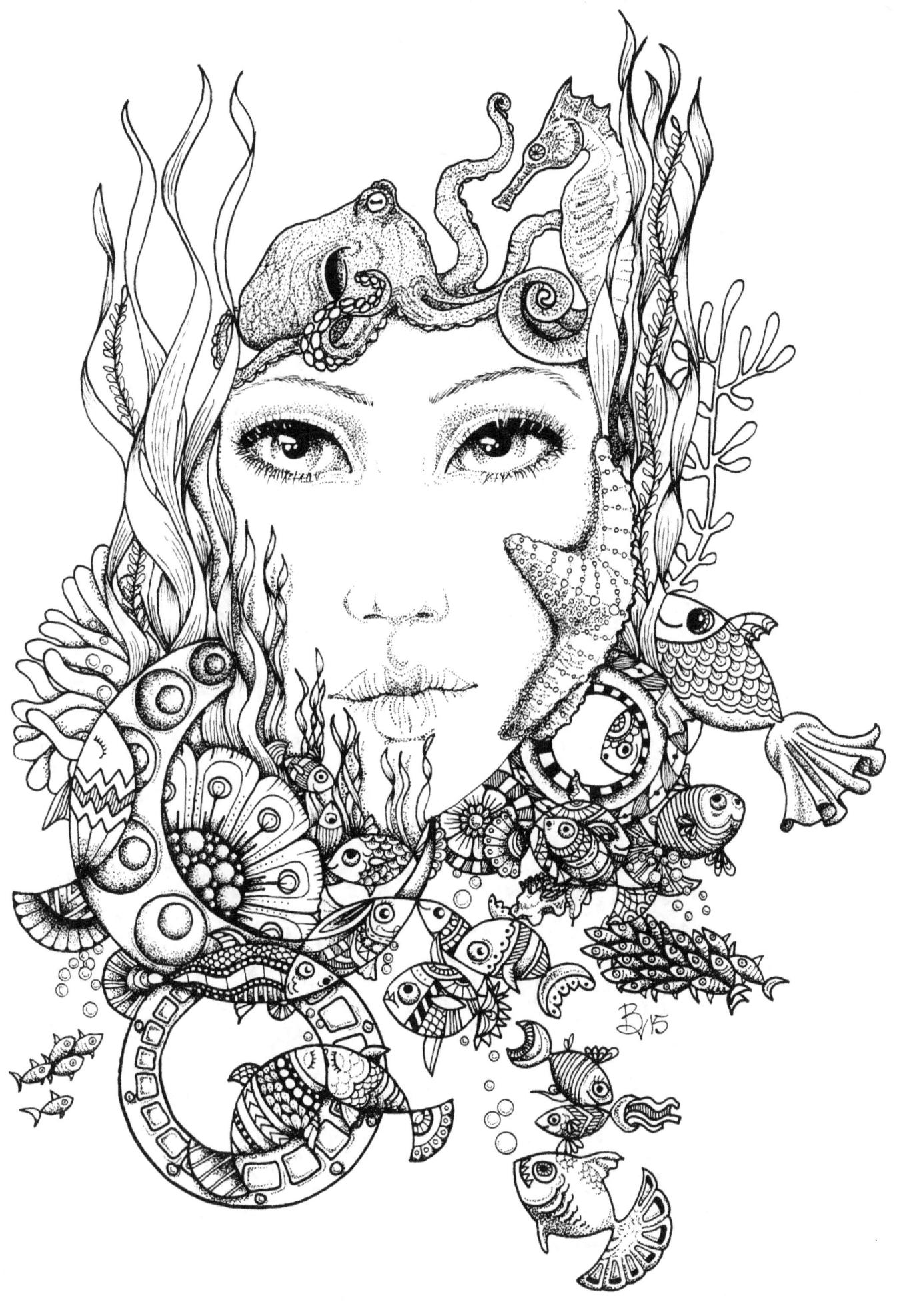

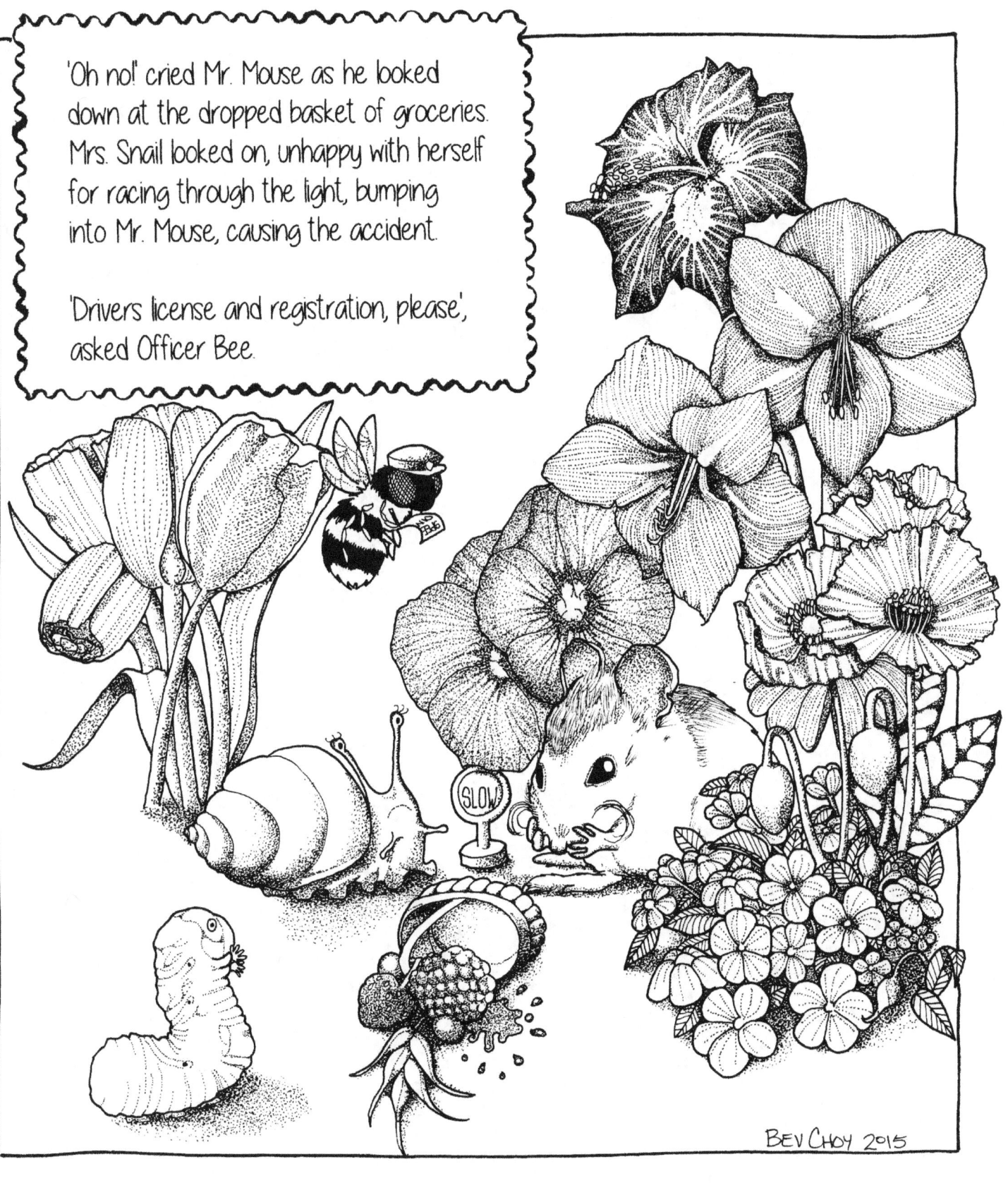

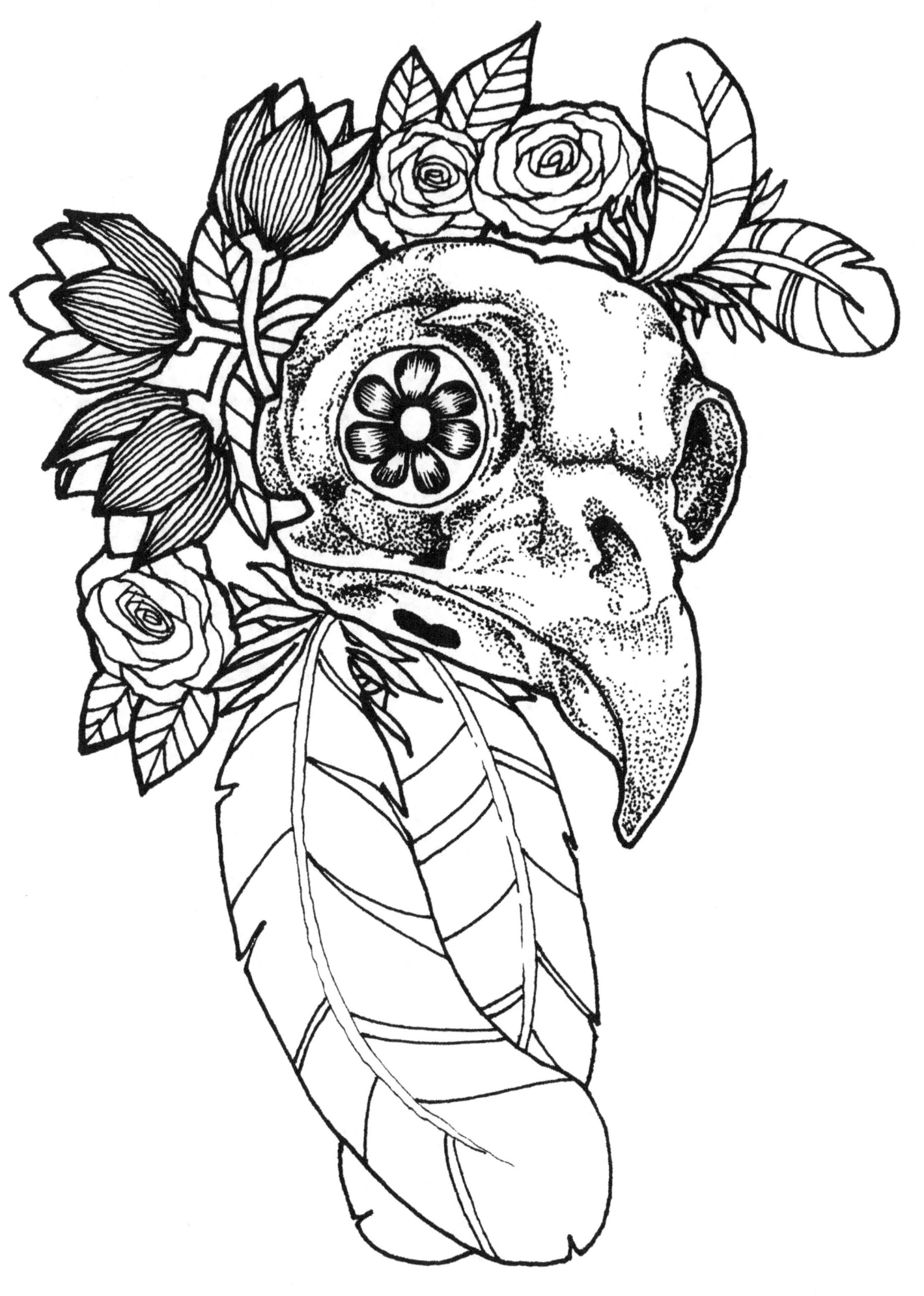

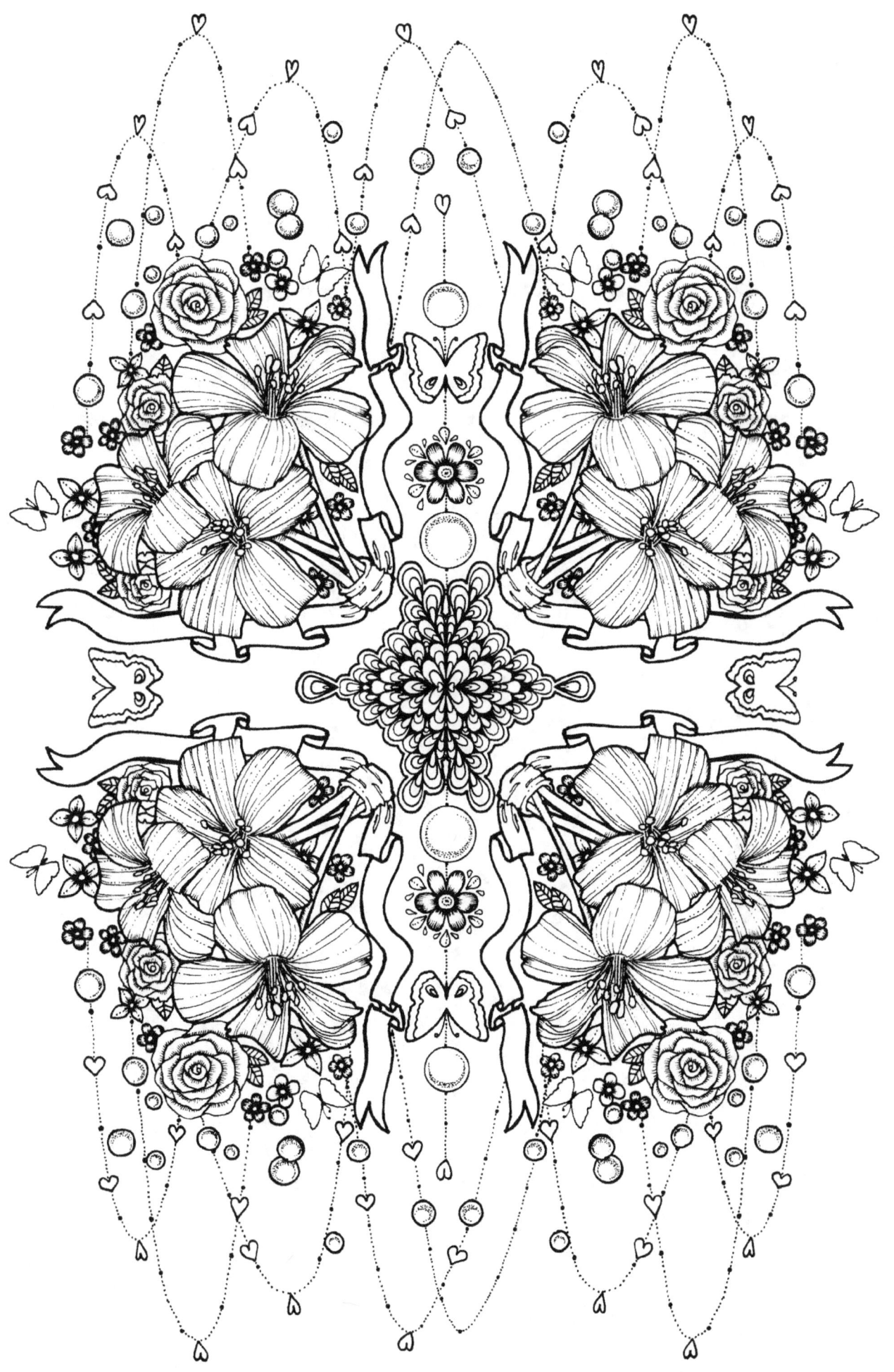

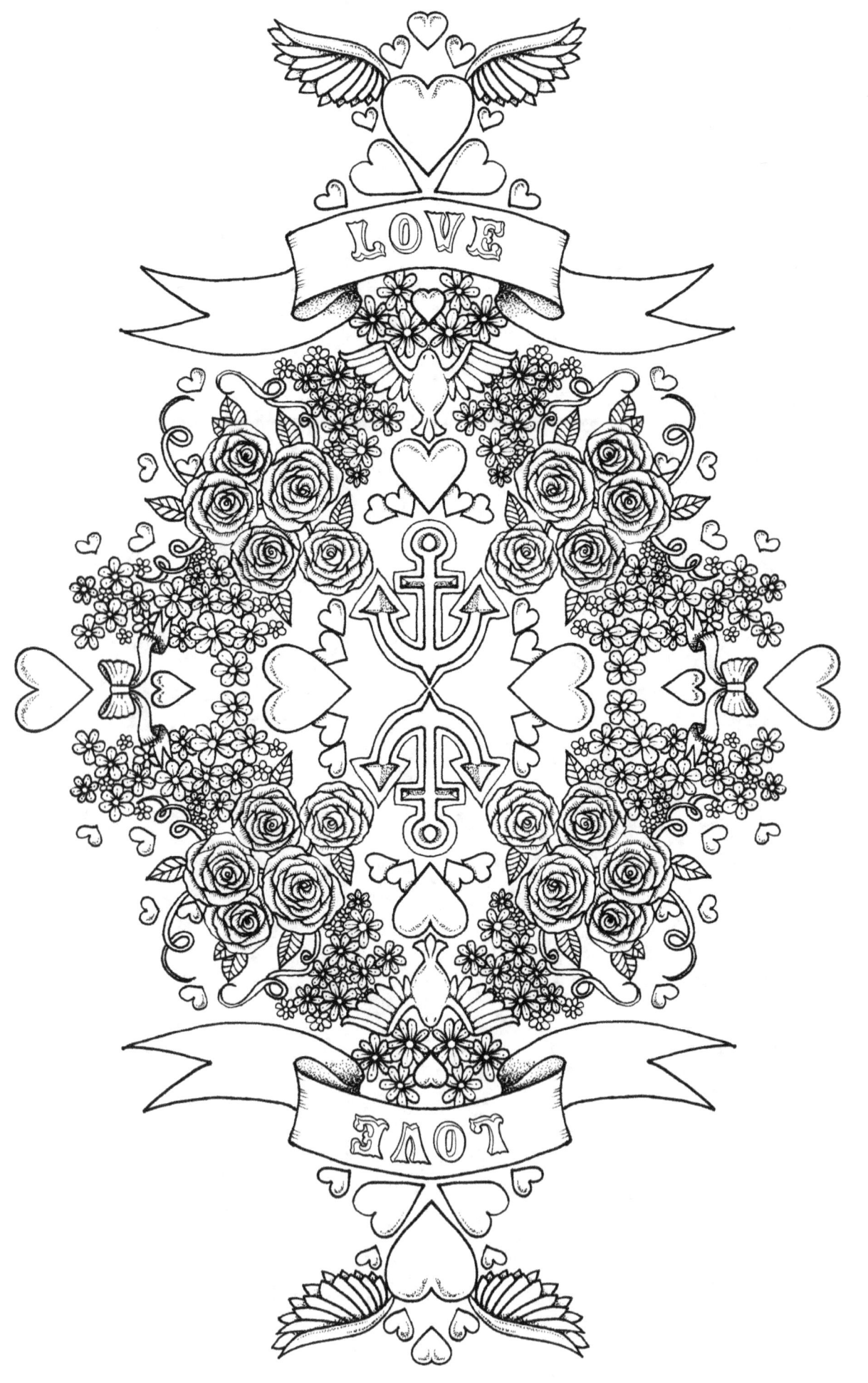

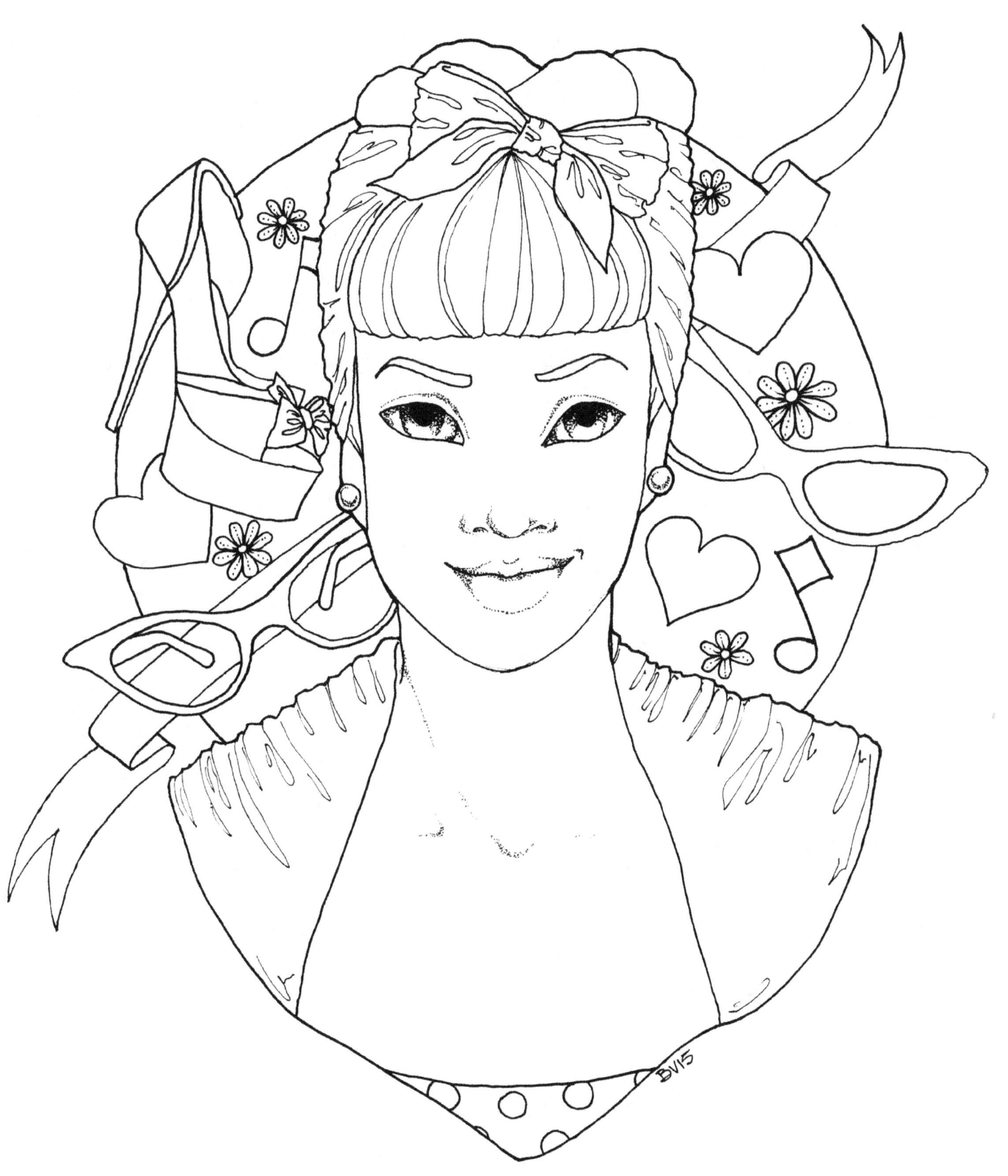

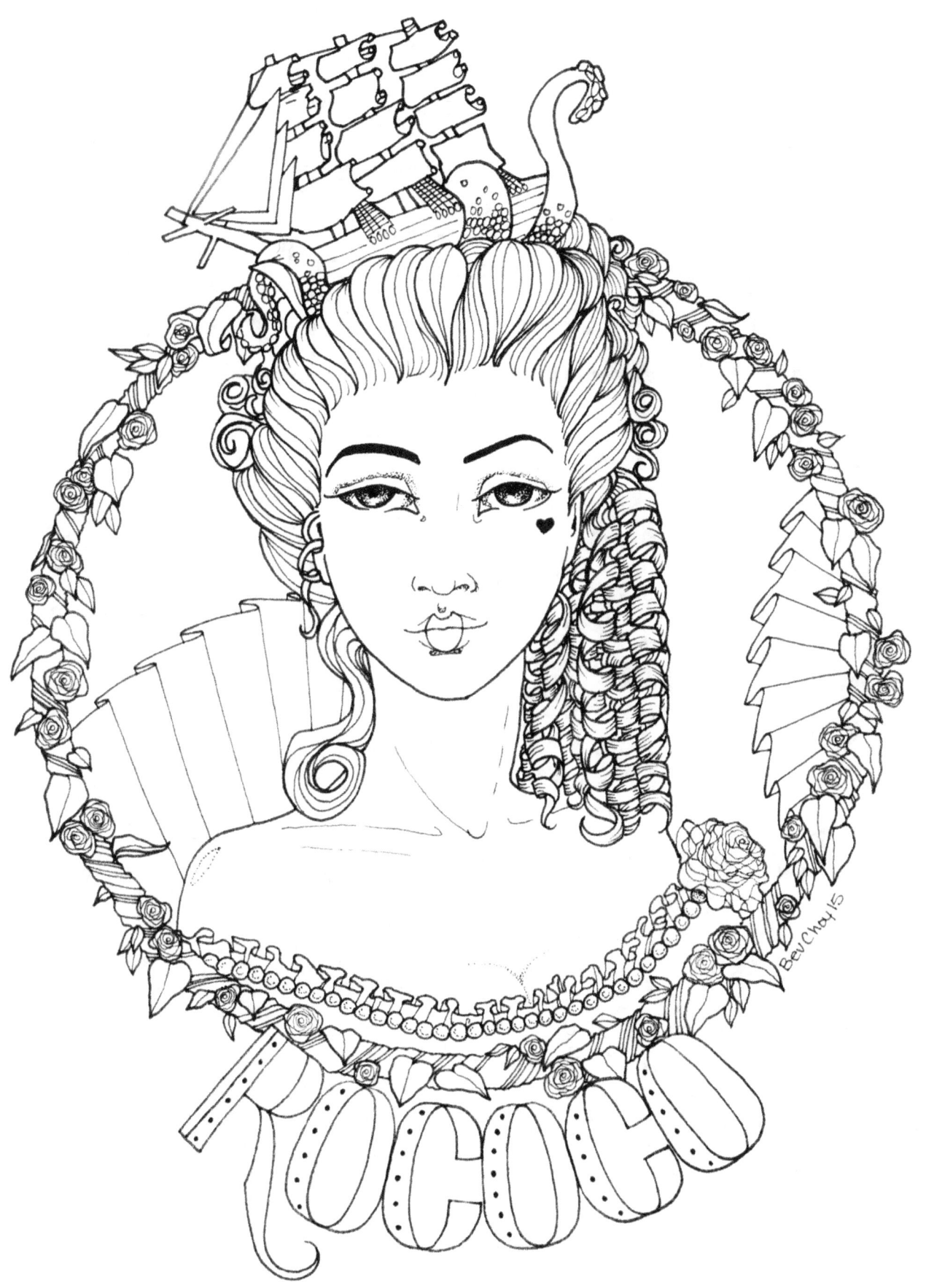

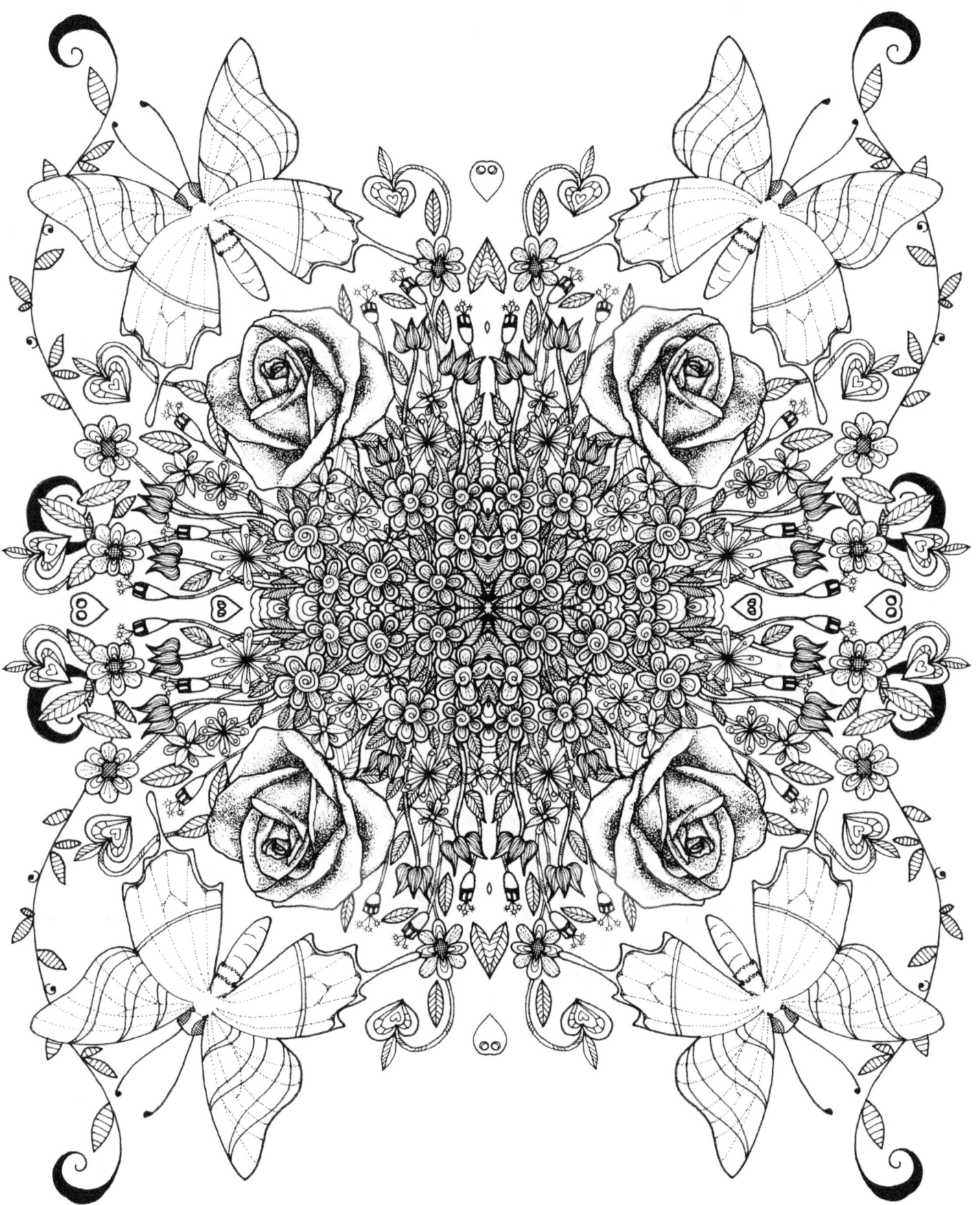

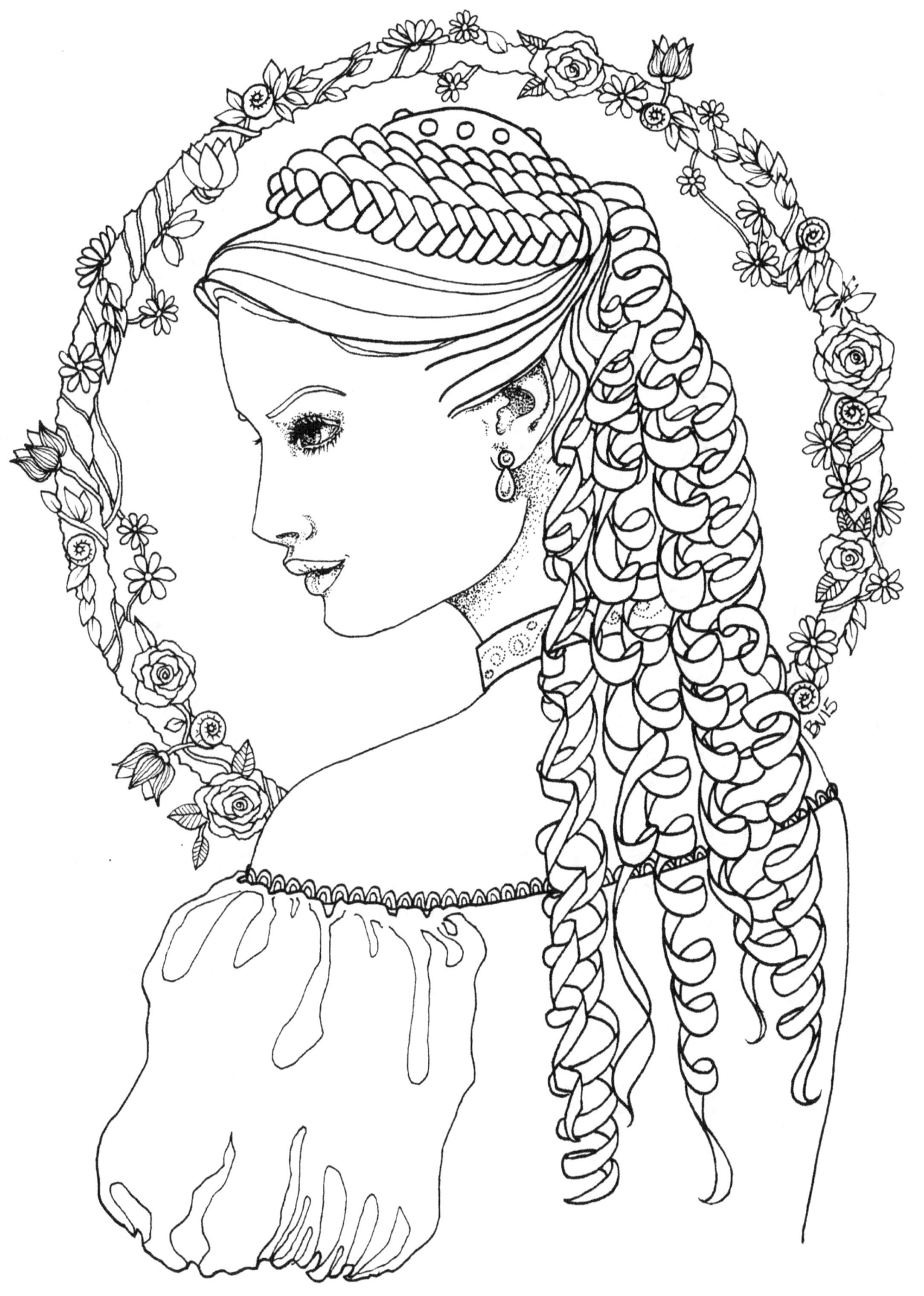

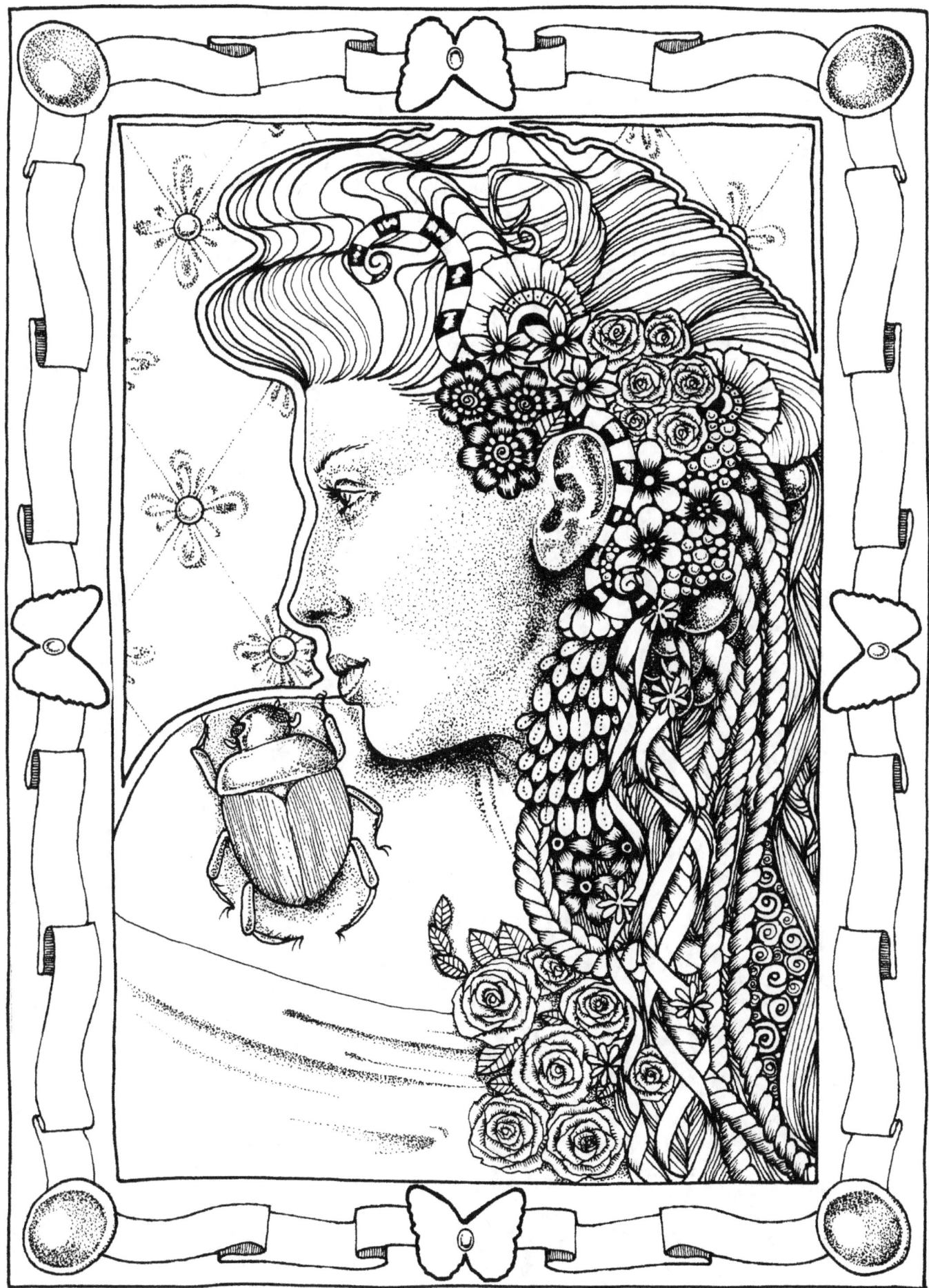

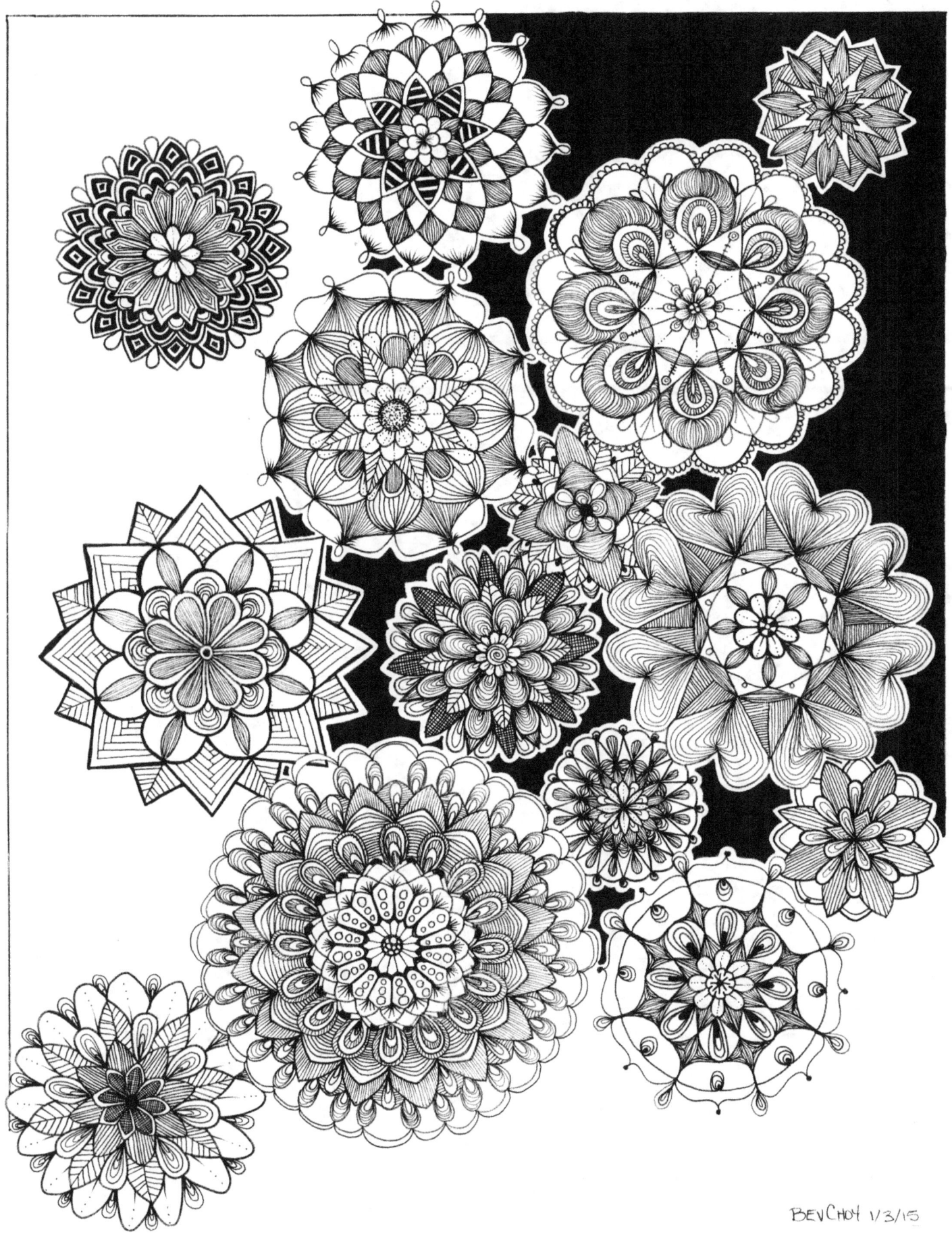

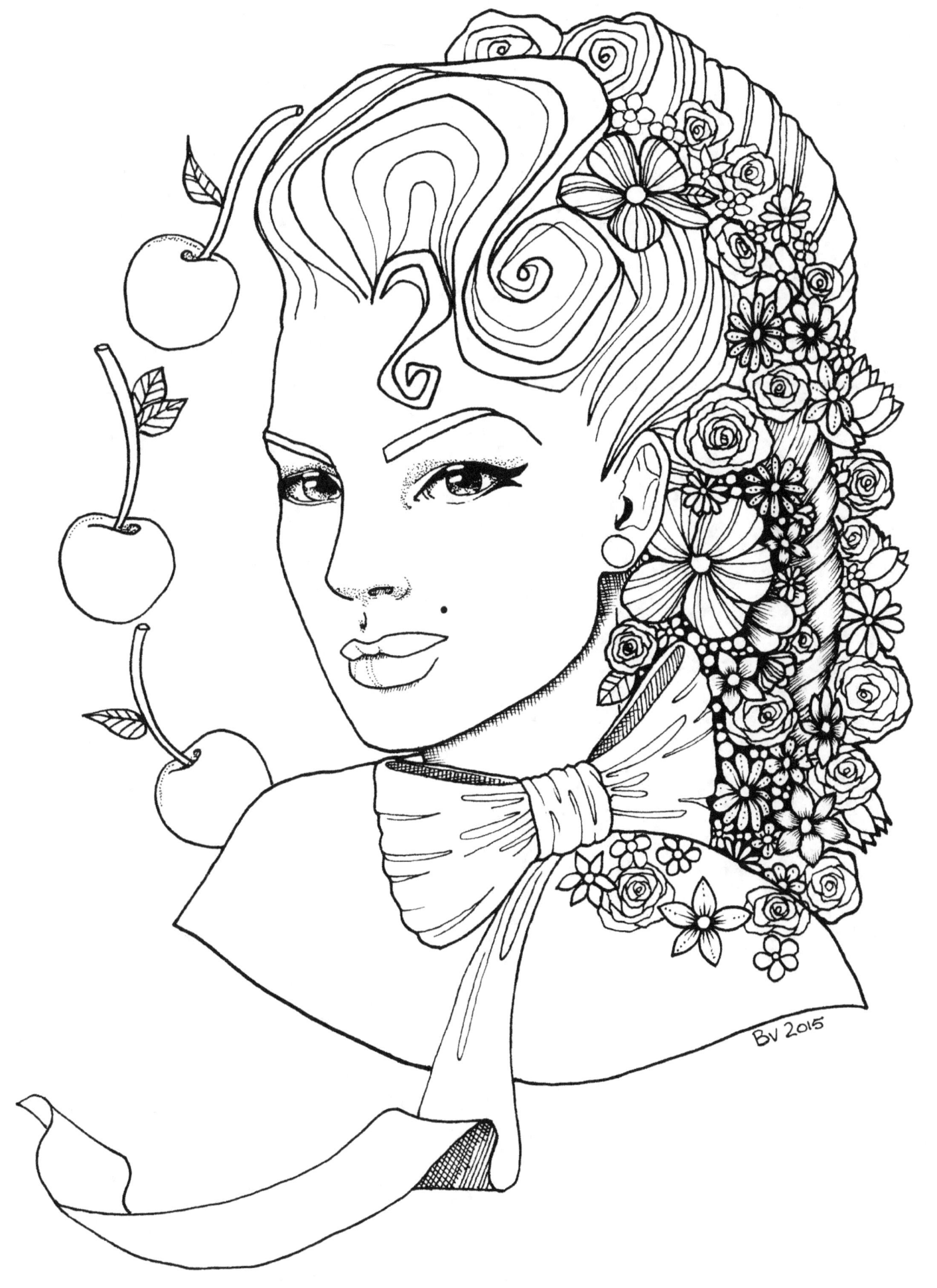

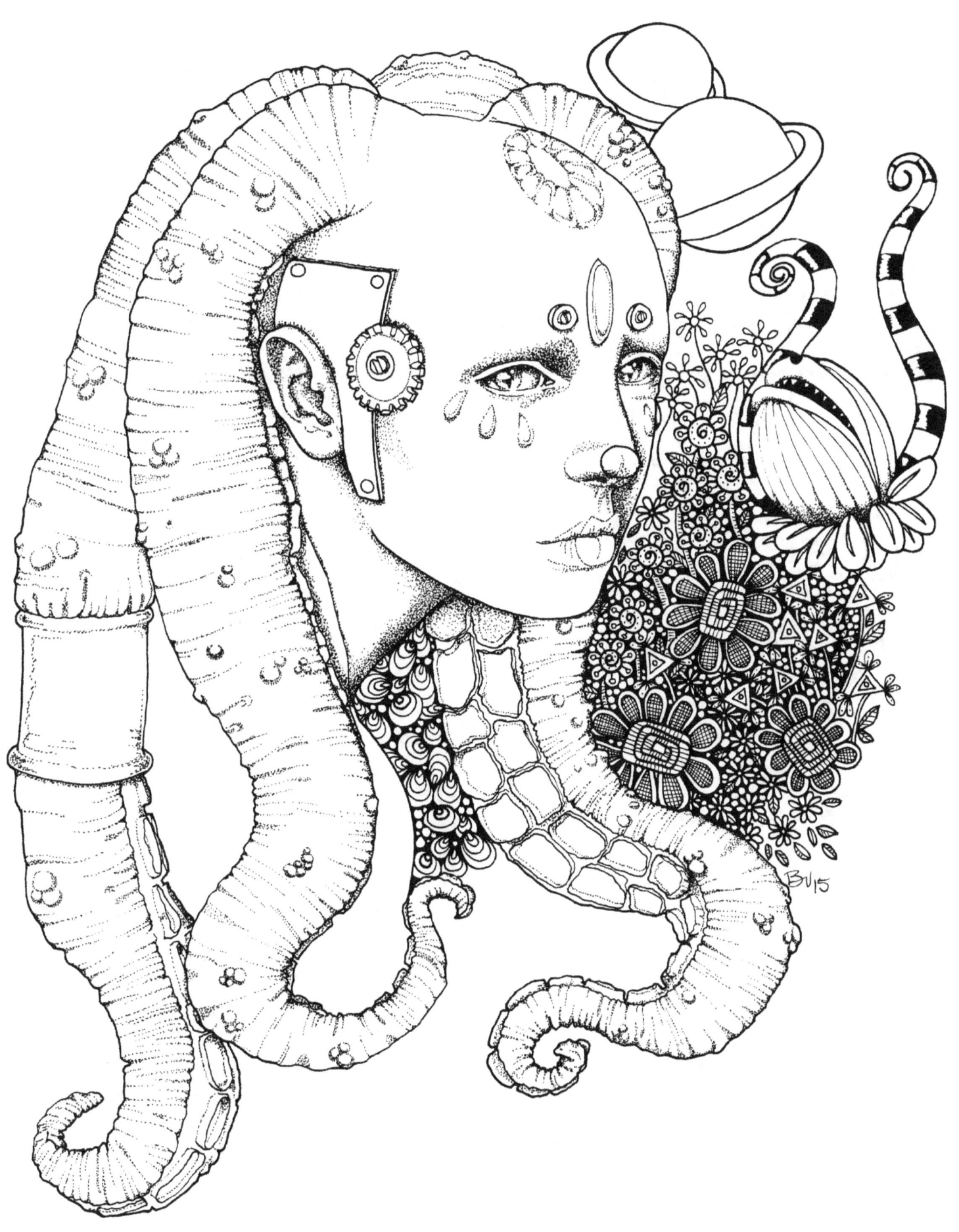

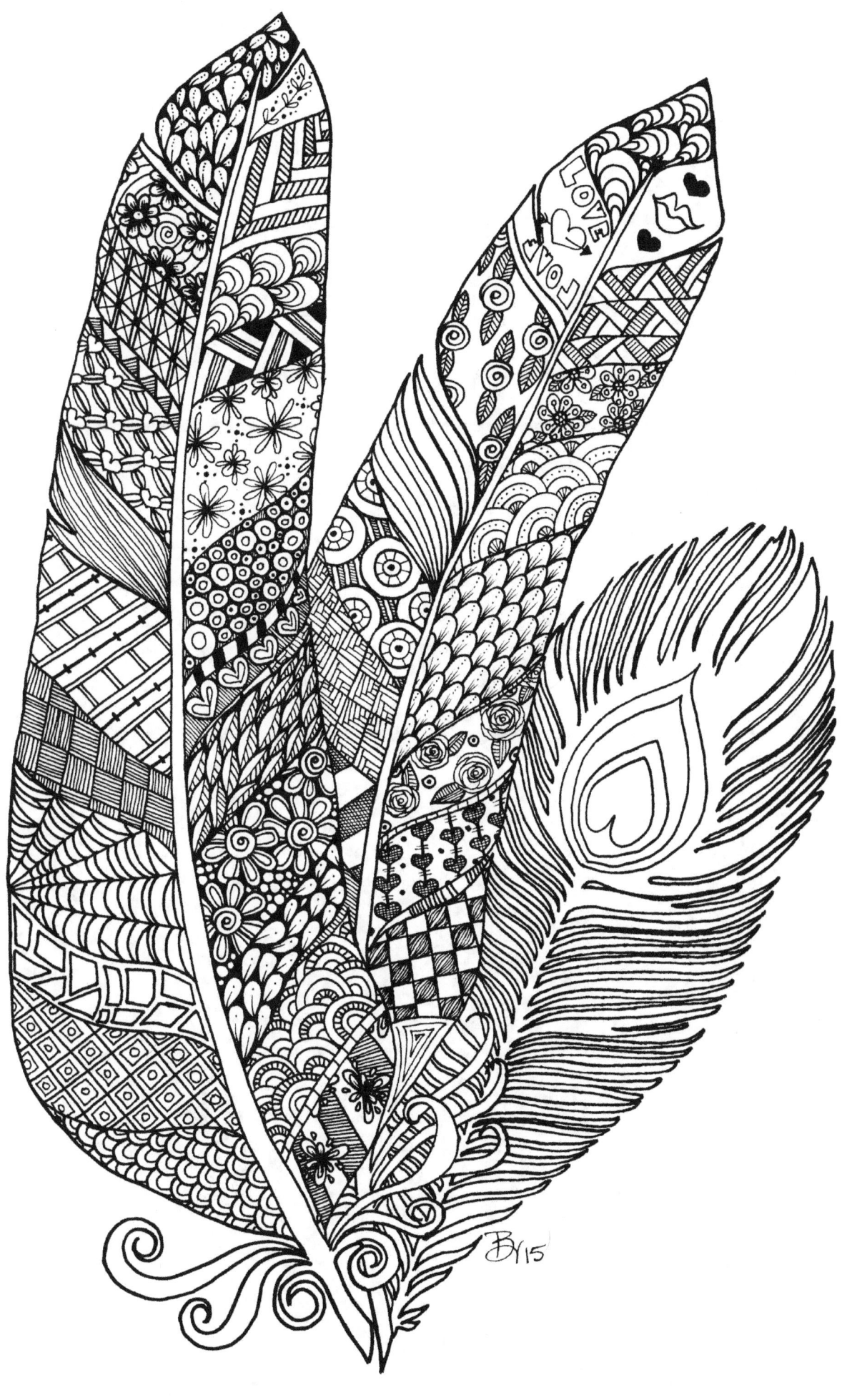

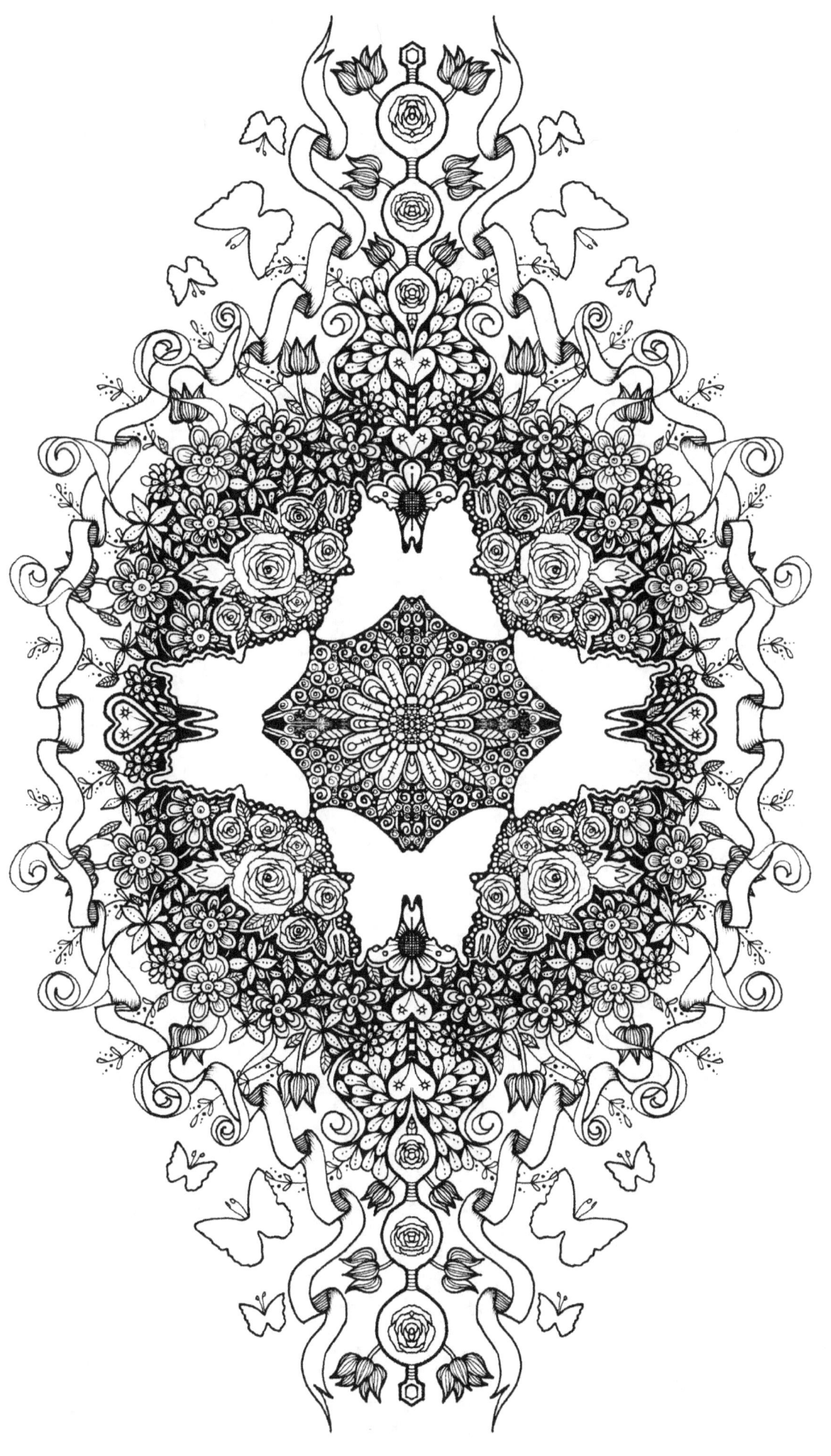

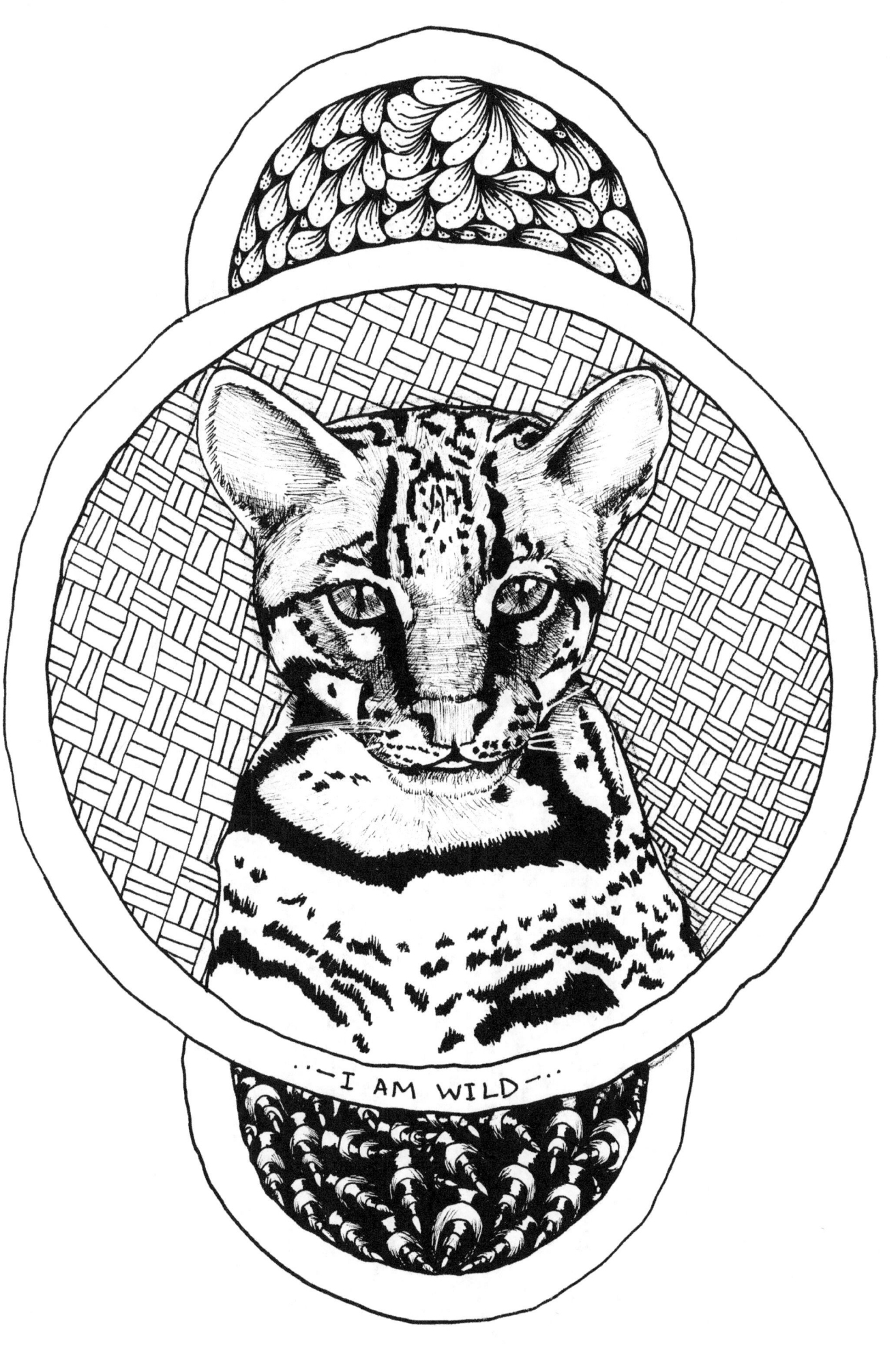

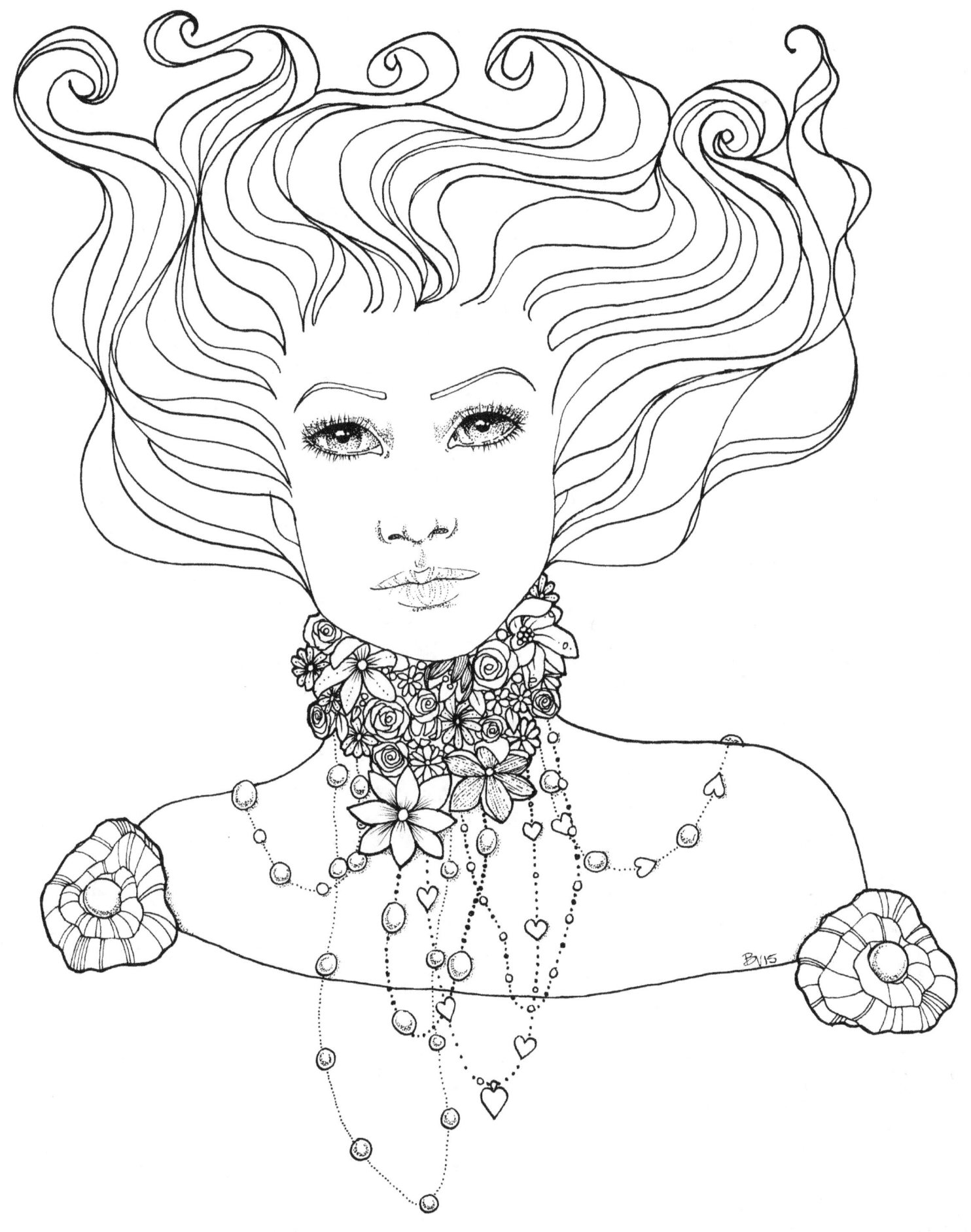

www.ingramcontent.com/pod-product-compliance
Lightning Source LLC
Chambersburg PA
CBHW082217220526
45470CB00010B/3209